THE TRUTH AS TOLD BY

MASON BUTTLE

ALSO BY LESLIE CONNOR

FOR MIDDLE GRADE READERS
All Rise for the Honorable Perry T. Cook
Waiting for Normal
Crunch

FOR YOUNGER READERS
Miss Bridie Chose a Shovel

FOR TEENS
Dead on Town Line
The Things You Kiss Goodbye

THE TRUTH AS TOLD BY
MASON BUTTLE

Leslie Connor

 KATHERINE TEGEN BOOKS
An Imprint of HarperCollins Publishers

Katherine Tegen Books is an imprint of HarperCollins Publishers.

The Truth as Told by Mason Buttle

Library of Congress Control Number: 2017934896
ISBN 978-0-06-249143-5

Typography by Carla Weise
19 20 21   CG/LSCH   20 19 18 17 16 15 14 13 12
❖
First Edition

FOR MAC AND JESS AND SAM AND IAN,
BROTHERS AND SONS.
YOU ARE THE BEST BOYS I KNOW.

chapter 1

THE STOOPID SHIRT

Tell you what. I already know who stuffed this T-shirt into my locker. Matt Drinker did that. He took a Sharpie to it first. Fat black letters. He wrote STOOPID on it. Same way I spelled my word in the spelling bee on Friday morning.

A kid like me does not belong in the spelling bee. But it is for all of seventh grade. This is not how I would kick off the school year, but I'm not in charge. Elimination rounds start in the classrooms.

I'm eliminated.

I saw a movie about a spelling bee once. There was a girl, and she had a magic about her. She could hear her word—any word at all—and the letters wrote themselves in the air. It happened in swirls and sparkles with fuzzy bees and fairies making glitter trails. The letters opened like apple blossoms. They flowed like paint off a brush. Always the *right* letter.

People said that couldn't really happen, seeing things that way. It was just a movie trick. But I believe what that girl saw. At least some.

I see things too. But no fairy wings. No flowers blooming.

Here is what happened on Friday morning: I heard my word.

Stopped.

Had to be the easiest word ever in a seventh-grade spelling bee. Tell you what. I knew I was going to spell it right. *Stopped* has double letters. I like those. It is like getting a two for one. Well, too bad, because as soon as I thought of that, I thought of another word. Starts with the same sound and has double letters somewhere around the middle part.

Stoop.

I have been with my brain for twelve long years. I know how it puts things wrong. So I closed my eyes. I thought, okay, Mason, don't let that in your head. Don't go spelling *stoop.* That's not your word. Your word is *stopped.* Under my eyelids I started to see the letters. That's why I say it is like the girl from the movie. I can *see* the letters. But for me they go ugly. They fade or swell up. They slide away. If my eyes had pinchers on them, I'd grab at the letters and hold them still.

Tick. Tick. Tick.

You cannot take your time in a spelling bee.

Stopped.

S and T.

Those were correct. I knew they were. I said them. I got the safe feeling. The spelling timer ticked again.

I tried to see the letters. Clear. But they fuzzed. Then they blobbed. I have seen it plenty of times.

I squeezed my eyes shut tighter. I thought, please let me get this. I saw fat letters. Blurry letters. Then came the other thing I see. Color. Happens sometimes. This time it was the dirty green. Floats in like smoke. Happens when I can't get to the right answers. That green, it is the color of pressure. On me. A spelling bee is pressure.

I rolled my eyeballs behind my lids. Tried to erase all that mess. My brain got itself caught on that other word: *stoop.* Double letters.

Tick. Tick.

I saw two Os.

I said two Os.

Somebody snorted.

I knew I was wrong. Knew I had to finish. Get it over with. I wiped my sweaty hands on my pants. *Stopped.* I heard a P sound. I said it quick. Knew there was something more. T on the end? No! D! It would be D on the end. But not just D . . .

Tick. Tick. No time.

I said, "I and D."

What I spelled was S-T-O-O-P-I-D.

What it sounded like was *stupid.*

The buzzer sounded. That whole classroom roared.

Matt Drinker loves when something like that happens. That's why I'm guessing he put this STOOPID shirt inside my locker. He must have picked my lock to do it. Funny thing is I knew what the shirt said because of the two Os in the middle. I knew in two blinks.

Matt doesn't know it but he did me a big favor. I always take two shirts to school. Unless I forget. I change just before lunch. This is because of how I sweat. It is a lot. Can't stop it. Can't hide it. I need to be dry at the lunch table. Otherwise I'm a total gross-out of a kid.

Well, today was a day that I forgot my extra shirt. So I'm wearing this one that says STOOPID on it. It's big and it fits me. It's clean and dry. I'm going to keep moving. Maybe nobody will see what it says.

And if they do, well, tell you what. Plenty worse has happened.

chapter 2

THE SWOOF

O ther kids look up to me in the hallway. They have
to. I'm the biggest, tallest seventh grader at Merrimack Middle School. By a lot. Today, I'm moving fast.
They laugh when they see me. Laughing is better than no
laughing. I smile. I know I look funny. Like a big walking
billboard for STOOPID with two Os.

I'm skipping the cafeteria. It is a wild place. Seems like
a STOOPID shirt could start a food fight. I am headed to
the SWOOF. That's Ms. Blinny's room. I take giant steps
all the way down the hall. I think about this: The SWOOF
has double Os in the middle. Like the word on my shirt.

Funny name, the SWOOF. Ms. Blinny made that up.
She used some little tile letters. They came from a sign

that said SOCIAL WORK OFFICE. I know that because Ms. Blinny told me. She was making the SWOOF sign the day I met her. Mrs. Lorenz from the elementary school brought me over to the middle school on the last day of fifth grade so I could meet her friend.

We walked through the front part of the office where there is a big soft couch and two beanbag chairs. Also, a lava lamp and the little table with a snack basket on top. There are posters on the walls and a whole lot of clutter. Ms. Blinny's desk is the last thing, tucked behind a bookcase by the window.

Something smelled hot in there the day I went to meet Ms. Blinny. Sure enough, she was holding a glue gun in one hand and pushing those letter tiles around on her desk with the other. Pink paint was drying on a nice wooden shape. A pink paintbrush was drying onto her desk. Ms. Blinny sure was busy. But when she saw me, she looked up and smiled.

She said, "Oh yeah! Mason! Glad to meet you." The smile got bigger. She stayed looking at me—like a person shining from the inside out. *At me.* Her glue gun dripped a glob of hot stuff onto her papers.

I said, "Be careful!"

She said, "Oh! Oops! Dripping!" Then there went another string of glue. She grabbed for a tissue, but she spilled a tub of glitter beads across the desk. She smiled with a big open mouth and bright happy eyes. "Ha! Look at that, Mason. A sparkle spill!" She took a picture of it. That has been her screen saver for more than a year now.

There was a new SOCIAL WORK OFFICE sign on the door when school started last September. I mean the plain kind. Like the school puts up. But Ms. Blinny had finished her glitter project too. She stuck her pink SWOOF sign on the door. Tell you what. Makes the room easy to find.

I like the way she is, Ms. Blinny. How she spills things and doesn't wait for paint to dry.

So today, I turn the corner into her room. Breathe out a breath. The kind that means you made it home. I like the SWOOF. I am always welcome here.

chapter 3

BETTER THAN STOOPID

I'm the only kid in the SWOOF today. But I won't be for long. It's a stopping-in place. I poke my head around the bookcase. I tell Ms. Blinny hello. She is working. But I can interrupt her if I am polite about it. I hold up my lunch bag for her to see. I have twisted the top into a thing that looks like a pumpkin stem. It's wet from me sweating it up.

I say, "Okay if I eat in here?"

She says, "Sure!" She pushes a button on her desk phone. She tells the office, "Hello. I have Mason Buttle and I'm *keeping* him for a while." She says *keeping* as if everyone should want to keep me.

At the end of the call, Ms. Blinny stands. She is small

even in her tall boots. She looks up to me too. She tilts her head. She is reading my shirt. The letters that spell STOOPID. She says, "Mason? Want to tell me about the shirt?"

I look at my chest. Ms. Blinny might already know about the spelling bee. She knows lots of things about me.

I won't tell that I think it was Matt Drinker who put the shirt in my locker and I won't tell why either. I say, "It's clean and dry. It's handmade."

She says, "Handmade . . . hmmm. I don't like it. It's *derogatory.*"

I shrug. *Derogatory* must be bad. But what am I going to do about it anyway? My morning shirt is all sweated up. It's in a bag inside my locker.

Ms. Blinny opens her desk drawer. Pulls out a roll of duct tape. The decoration kind. Purple plaid. She pulls off two strips. Tapes over STOOPID like she is crossing that off me. Then she takes out a Sharpie of her own. She says, "Mind if I write on you, Mason?"

I tell her, "Go ahead."

Being written on is tricky. Ms. Blinny has me tuck a copy of the *Merrimack Gazette* up the front of my shirt. I look down and watch her write. She puts three words.

There's a thing to know about me: I can barely read. I can't read right side up and I sure cannot read upside down. But now she is drawing a picture too. She draws two squares with corners overlapping. Connects the sides with four lines. I know this one. It is a box.

Ms. Blinny finishes. She backs up. She puts the cap on her Sharpie. Good thing, because she's tapping the end of the marker on her bottom lip now. She smiles. Big white teeth. She says, "Wait, wait! I just thought of something else." She pops the pen open again.

She writes two more upside-down words. Puts a question mark on the end. She says, "Done!" I peel the *Merrimack Gazette* out from under my shirt. The front page is wet from my sweat. We agree that I should put that in the recycle bin, and I do.

I tug on the bottom of the shirt. Look down the long front of me. I ask Ms. Blinny, "What do I say now?"

She reads. "THINKS OUTSIDE THE . . ." Then she points to her drawing. Looks up at me.

I say, "Box?"

She says, "Yes!" Then she reads the last part. "CAN YOU?" She chirps that part like a bird. She says, "Your shirt makes a statement *and* asks a question. It is a curiosity!" She smiles, Sharpie waving in the air.

I nod. I say, "Guess that's better than STOOPID. Just one thing, Ms. Blinny. What does it mean?"

She says, "Thinking outside the box is a skill. It means your mind is big and open, Mason. If you can think outside the box, you have no limits! That's you!" Ms. Blinny is smiling. *At me.*

I say, "And it is not *derogatory*."

She says, "Not one bit."

I run through that again. THINKS OUTSIDE THE BOX. Memorize it.

She says, "Okay. Get comfy and have your lunch, Mason. Oh, and think about some of the things you and I always talk about. Let your mind go deep. When you're done eating, I have something new for you to try."

I choose the one hard chair in the SWOOF. I can dry it off later if I sweat it up. I untwist the top of my lunch bag. Wonder what Ms. Blinny has planned. Wonder if my mind can be deep.

Then I think this: Well, I guess my mind can be outside a box. Maybe that's a start.

chapter 4

OUR PLACE

When I say that Ms. Blinny knows a lot about me, I mean she knows because I tell her. She says I talk a blue streak. She thinks I have a story. Funny thing. She is not the only one who thinks that. Lieutenant Baird thinks it too. He thinks I have a story about my best friend, Benny Kilmartin. More than I already told him. He gave me that notebook. Wants me to write in it. But that is a nightmare for a kid like me.

Ms. Blinny means a different story. More like the whole thing about me. My story. She talks about that like it's something I'm sitting on. Like I could pull it out from under me. Like a copy of the *Merrimack Gazette*. Like any old time now, I will say, *Here. Here's the true story of* me. *Mason Buttle.*

Some people might think they already know my story. That's just because they live around here. Some stuff is plain. Some stuff is right where you can see it.

If you lived in Merrimack you might know our place. It's the crumbledown house out on Swaggertown Road. Sits on a good bit of acres that used to be a whole lot more. Developers. My uncle Drum says we can't live without them. My grandma says we should have tried.

You might know our orchard. You might remember it looking alive as a hive late in summer. PYO. Pick Your Own.

If you are like me your eyes about pop out of your head at how quick the developers dozered down the trees. They are still building. New houses. Up the hill and down the hill from our place. You might look at our house sitting in the middle and wonder why it looks like somebody emptied a dustpan over it.

I try. I sweep up the porch. Pull weeds in the front. But I am *now and then* about it. I don't keep up. Uncle Drum says just leave it. Then another shingle drops off the roof. Lands in the yard.

But that crumbledown is still home. The place I start from every day. If I had a story it might begin there. But tell you what. It would not be long before I got to the parts that could ruin anybody's lunch.

I sit in the SWOOF staring at my sandwich. Not eating. Must be my mind has gone deep.

I think this: Benny Kilmartin *is* a part of my story. Best friends since first grade. The Kilmartin place is not far down the road from my house. Walking distance. I went to Benny's house a lot. And he came to mine. Like brothers with two homes. So I got close with Benny's dads. Andy is the most at-home dad. A carpenter. A housepainter. Benny's other dad is Franklin. He works in an office in the city. But it was Andy who always watched for the bus. So I miss him. But most of all, I miss Benny.

Benny's been gone since the end of fifth grade. Springtime. Apple-blossom time. That's a year. Plus a few months. He died in May and now it is the second September since. Second bloom. Second apple time. I think of the apples because Benny died in the orchard. Our orchard.

That's the story Lieutenant Baird wants. I already told him. I told everyone. I found Benny still as a stone right under the tree fort. I saw the ladder was broken. Top rung snapped. Hanging. Saw that just before I tried to make Benny Kilmartin breathe again. I guess it was not the best ladder. I told everyone that I was sorry about that. I wish I'd built that better. But that ladder was not broken at suppertime when I jumped down from the tree fort. Heading for home. I got no idea what made that rung give out. I didn't then. And I don't now.

So now you know it. My best friend is dead.

Tell you what. Puts a fly in my head thinking about what happened to Benny Kilmartin.

chapter 5

TALK TO THE DRAGON

I look at my lap. Got the end of my sandwich sitting there. I don't want it. My lunch seems pretty ruined. I ball that up with the bag. I mop dry with two napkins as best I can. The sweating is always ahead of the mopping with me. I look up. So far, I'm still the only kid in the SWOOF.

A swish and thud come from behind the bookcase where Ms. Blinny is. Happens a lot. I don't worry too much. She usually says what has happened right after it happens. Things like, "Oh, spilled my purse." "Oops, knocked over the pothos plant."

Today she says, "Uh-oh, my planner . . . and my papers." I can hear her sweep them off the floor. She pops her head around the bookcase. She says, "Done with lunch, Mason? Good! Come on back here. I have something for you to try."

She sits me at a small desk that is pushed up against a wall opposite her bigger desk. My knees come up tall underneath it. Lift it some. The small desk is new this year. She opens a laptop in front of me. That's new too. She brings up a program. I think this: Is she going to ask me to read?

But then I know she won't. She knows how it is with me. Ms. Blinny untangles a headset and puts it on. There's a little mic on a wire at her mouth. Her eyes are wide. She says, "Watch this, Mason." She speaks. She says, "Wake up." Then she says, "Hello, Dragon. Meet Mason."

I think, Dragon? I am not a third grader. I watch. But only because I like Ms. Blinny.

Then I see it. Words type themselves on the screen. Ms. Blinny points at them. She tells the Dragon, "Stop listening." She brings her hands together with a clap. She says, "See that? I tell it to stop listening so it won't think I'm still writing when I'm talking to you." She says, "You'll learn the commands. But look!" She points at the screen again.

I look at the words. They go all floaty. Like always. But I see one word that I know by the shape of it. My name. On the end. Letter M. That's right. I heard Ms. Blinny say it: *Meet Mason.*

She gives me the headset. She says, "Your turn. Talk to

the Dragon! Start by telling it to wake up."

So I put on that headset. I gulp. Two times. I tug at the wires. Stare at the screen. Finally, I say, "Wake up." Then I say, "Y-you don't look like a dragon."

I hear tiny clicks. Typing sounds. The words line up across the screen. My eyes open wide. I think I see my sentence. Maybe even spelled right.

Ms. Blinny tells me, "Now say *play back* and listen."

I do that. A lady-voice comes through the earphones: "You-you don't look like a dragon."

I say, "Holy cow!"

The Dragon types two words. So then I say, "Play back."

The lady-voice says, "Holy cow."

Ms. Blinny takes tiny running steps in place. Happy boots. She twirls around. She says, "Is that cool or what? You can pick a font. And a color if you want to."

I think this: Best part is, I don't have to look at the screen at all. I don't have to read it. Don't have to think about letter sounds. No wishing for pincher eyes to hold the letters in place. No blinking to clear a mess.

Ms. Blinny says, "Those are your words. You're writing, Mason! Come do it every day. This can be your journal. It's the story of *you*. You can use it to dump all the stuff that's on your mind." She makes her voice gruff. "Feed it to the Dragon," she says. She pumps her arms over her head. "Yay!"

In my head I remember what one teacher told me: *If you can talk, you can write.*

I told that teacher, *No. If you can talk, you can tell a story. But you still might not be able to write it.*

It was no wisecrack. It was a true thing. I can start the writing. But it is not as fast as talking. I get lost. There is only one way to get back on track and that is to read what I already wrote. But for me, the reading is the trouble.

Now I know Ms. Blinny is right. The Dragon will let me talk out a story. This should be good. Easier. But here I sit. Frozen at the Dragon.

Ms. Blinny sees me being stuck. She says, "Whatever you were thinking about while you were eating your lunch, start there."

I think this: Well. Maybe some of it.

She says, "Just be yourself while you are at the Dragon."

So I do that. The Dragon types. And then I know it. If I have a story this is the way for me to tell it. As best I can.

chapter 6

MORNINGS

I start my story from home. I tell this to the Dragon:

Umm. Okay. I umm. I get on the bus. I have a seat to
myself. Most mornings. More kids use the bus in the
afternoon. Depends on the day. But in the morning most
get a ride. So umm yeah. The day starts quiet. And I like
being up high. Looking out the window. On my own. Then I
don't worry that I'm sweating against someone. I just watch
outside. I have checkpoints along the loop through town.

I stop. I think. How do I tell this? Is this even a real
story? Then I remember *sequence*. That is the order. The

order of how things happen. I rest my head on my hands.
I don't look at the screen. I tell the Dragon:

First. Umm. Umm. Okay I know. First comes the commuter
lot. That's at Town Hall. I watch for the men. Saw four or
five this morning. Work boots on. Paper-cup coffees in their
hands. I wish Uncle Drum would wait with them instead
of heading to the diner every morning like he does. See
those guys they do get work. The contractors from the
new neighborhoods pick them up. Pay them to dig or lift.
Help out. Not every day I guess but some days. I bet the
pay is enough to make a difference at their places. I hear
Grandma say it to Uncle Drum. The money from selling our
land is enough to live on now. But it won't last forever if we
keep picking from it.

I stop to think. I know I have been talking that blue
streak. The Dragon is writing. Everything. This is important. All the words are going to be somewhere. I think
about what to say. Then I speak again.

So. Umm. I love Uncle Drum. Maybe even extra since I had
a walk-away daddy. That's from before I can remember.
What I know is my mom moved us in to live with my
grandma and grandpa after that. Uncle Drum had never
left the place. So he was there for me. He used to bring
me to the diner in the mornings. Let me draw circles in the

syrup on his plate. Then lick my fingers. When I was big enough and umm I did get big pretty quick he took me all through our orchard on the tractor. He fixed a wooden box right behind the driver's seat for me. That's still on there. If I tried to sit in it now I'd break it. Or get my butt stuck in it. Umm. So. I think it is not all his fault that he gave up on the orchard. We had the bad year. I was six. Yeah. Six years old. Gramps died. Then Mom died. Bing. Bang. That's how Uncle Drum tells that. He ran the orchard alone. It is a big job and then tell you what. The crop was bad. Two years in a row. It can happen. Uncle Drum knows it. But when he talks about it now he says the place was burying him. The orchard sits now. What is left of it. And pretty much is still left.

The trees still make apples. Just keep on doing what they always did. It's apple season now. We have ripe ones. I'll do some picking. But not much will come of it. Not this year.

So. Yeah. I think about the crumbledown house. We need to do some work. Or use some of that money from the developers. And hire someone else to help fix things up. Seems like Uncle Drum doesn't want to do that. Costs a lot. I know. I think of it when I see the men at the commuter lot.

So. It's still warm now. But we had one winter. Maybe two years ago. And you wouldn't believe it could happen but it snowed right into our living room. White stripe on the rug. Just the one. And I still had my best friend Benny. Then. So his dad Andy came. To help. Put up some shingles. Patched it. But tell you what. Another crack could open in that old roof. Anytime.

So. Uncle Drum hangs out at the diner. He gets his coffee poured by Irene in her hairnet. Stewart makes him a stack of corn cakes. I get that. I like to eat too. But Uncle Drum stays there for hours. Every day. All his clothes smell like bacon and maple syrup. Cab of his truck too. He doesn't take me with. Not anymore. But I see his truck parked in front when the bus takes me through. If the light is right I can see him inside. Sitting at the counter.

I have some idea about Uncle Drum's life being not quite filled up. Eating corn cakes is not a job. More like it's something to do if you don't want to do anything else. Like what you need to do. Uncle Drum doesn't say but I think he feels bad. But anyone who knows him would tell you he is a good guy. Some might say he's too good on account of how he brought Shayleen home that morning. Shayleen who took over my bedroom. Shayleen who drives me nuts. Shayleen who won't leave.

I stop talking when I get to this part about Shayleen. That's not surprising. Though it would feel pretty all right to keep going. Feed Shayleen to the Dragon. I laugh about that. I push back my chair. I look at the screen and see all the typing. Lines and lines. Can hardly believe it all. Then the letters begin to swell up. Turn splotchy. I blink and look away.

Behind me. The SWOOF has filled up with kids. Stopping in. I will have trouble keeping my brain on this. Ms. Blinny sees. She knows. She says, "All done for today, Mason? Great. Tell the Dragon to go to sleep. That's the command to use when you're finished."

So I do that. I dry my hands on my pants and pull the headset off. I use tissues to dry the earphones. Can't be a gross-out.

I have a wild feeling in me. Something new.

I have a lot more to say.

More to *write*.

chapter 7

TWO PRETZELS

The first rule about the SWOOF is that you are always welcome. Another rule is you cannot stay all day. Ms. Blinny will touch her heart with her hand and say, "Sorry. I'm not allowed to keep you forever."

Someday I will tell her that it doesn't make sense. How can you always be welcome if sometimes you cannot stay?

The bell is about to ring. I will have to go along to class. I get my tall knees out from under the desk. Close the lid of the laptop.

When I turn to leave I hear a hi. I look around. It's like that hi came out of the couch in the SWOOF. Then I see the kid. He is nothing but a pair of shoes and a fluffy white head. Kitten hair. The shoes are the desert-boot kind. Tan-sandy color. Can't see the rest of him because the big soft couch is swallowing up the whole middle of him. I can tell he's small. And thin. Looks like someone made him out of paper clips and Scotch tape.

He's looking up at me. Way up. I'm thinking about that hi. It was not a smiling hi. Not an I-don't-really-mean-it hi. Not a hi with so much air behind it that you'd never believe it was real. Just a plain hi. Like, you belong here as much as I belong here and you'll get no trouble from me.

He goes back to tapping around on a tablet in his lap. Well, if he even has a lap. I can't tell. Then he holds up a package of pretzels in his free hand. Jiggles the bag. Twice.

"Oh, for me?" I ask him.

"Of course," he says.

I dry my sweaty hand on my pants—three swipes— before I take one of the pretzels. I say, "Thank you."

He nods.

"I'm Mason," I tell him. Then I add, "Buttle."

He looks up again just long enough that I see him smile. I know that Buttle is a funny name. He looks back down at his tablet. He says, "Of course you are. And I'm Calvin Chumsky. I ride your bus." His smile grows out one side of his mouth. "Buttle and Chumsky," he whispers. I hear a little snort come out of him.

The bell rings. I tell him, "I have to go."

He nods. He says, "One for the road?" Shakes his pretzel bag again.

I take another. I thank him. I start for the door.

He says, "Hey, curious shirt by the way."

I look at my chest. Upside-down words.

I think. What is it again? Then I remember.

THINKS OUTSIDE THE picture of a box. CAN YOU?

I tell Calvin Chumsky, "Yeah. It is. Curious."

chapter 8

BIG YELLOW CHIPS

While I'm eating Calvin Chumsky's pretzel in the hall I think this: Been a long time since another kid offered me something to eat. Unless I count the time Matt Drinker and Lance Pierson got me to eat dog treats at the lunch table. They give me some trouble, Matt and Lance. Stuff like this STOOPID shirt. But they don't mean anything by it. Not really.

Man, they had a laugh about the dog treats. I didn't get it. I tried to say something polite about those big yellow chips. But they were horrible and hard. Made me check myself for a broken tooth.

I hid those chips in my sweaty hand. Pretended like

I had finished them up. When no one was looking I put them in the trash can.

All afternoon kids passed me in the hall saying, "Woof-woof! Bow-wow!" If they weren't barking, they were falling apart laughing. Made me laugh too. I didn't know what that was about. Not until I went down to Matt's house to take care of his dog, Moonie, a few days later. I do that when his family goes away. Matt lives in the house down a long hill from me. Through our orchard. His house is on part of the land that Uncle Drum sold to the developers. I love Matt's dog. Moonie. I like his house. Still smells new. And I like his mom. But I didn't like it much when I saw a box of those yellow chips in the Drinker pantry next to Moonie's dog food. Oh well. That's when I knew. I survived eating a dog treat. Tell you what. Worse can happen.

Anyway. Lucky thing to meet someone and know that you like them right away. And they like you. Used to happen more. Not as much now. But that is how it was when I met Ms. Blinny. And now with that little dude Calvin Chumsky with the pretzels. And going back a while it was like that with Matt's mom, Mrs. Drinker. She is a real friend of mine. A grown-up one. Been that way ever since I met her. That was the day I rode my sled in through her cellar window.

Tell you what. That is something that could have been all bad. But Mrs. Drinker turned it into good.

chapter 9

THE SLED

When the sled accident happened, Matt was the first one down his cellar stairs. He was pretty new in Merrimack. I already knew him from school. And the bus. And a few apple fights. Ones I didn't really want to be in. Already knew that it was his cellar I'd crashed into. His mom and his dog came down the stairs right behind him. Matt was yelling. His mom was gasping. And this black-and-white dog was looking at me all curious and wagging so hard. That's Moonie. He has the best tail that ever grew off the back of any dog.

I was apologizing as fast as I could and as many times as I could for breaking through the window and collapsing one end of the Drinkers' Ping-Pong table. Oh. And for denting their big white chest freezer. Tell you what. That sled sailed out from under me and hit it. I'm not sure how that happened. Must be about gravity or something.

I was trying to get up off the Ping-Pong table. Mrs. Drinker was begging me to stay down so she could look me over. Moonie must have thought *down* was meant for him because he dropped into that elbow-walking thing dogs do. He was trying to behave himself but still get to me.

Matt yelled at me, "Buttle! You idiot!"

I sat up.

Mrs. Drinker told me, "Wait, wait! Honey, does anything hurt? What about your head? And are you bleeding?"

Matt said, "You are *so* going to pay for that window, Buttle. And this Ping-Pong table too!"

"Matty!" Mrs. Drinker squawked at him. "This is a person who could be hurt! Let's not worry about objects!"

I touched my head, felt for my hat. Had that big pom-pom right on top. "I think I'm pretty okay," I said.

"Well, our house isn't!" Matt said. "There's damage. And you just trespassed too!"

I said, "Yeah . . . I made it around the apple trees. I thought I was going to be able to steer between the yards too. I don't know what happened." I shook my head, looked at the mess all around us. "Wow. Breaking and entering," I said.

That made Mrs. Drinker laugh.

"I am real sorry. I will pay for it. I will," I said. Then Mrs. Drinker looked ready to cry.

"Every last penny!" Matt said.

"Matty! Stop that!" Mrs. Drinker said, and then she really did sniffle. She put her arms around me. Then Matt's dog, Moonie, crawled up and he put his arms around me too.

They walked me home—Matt's dog and Matt's mom. She put on her boots and pulled my sled up the hill, even though I said I could do it. She wasn't having that. So, we walked and I reached down to pat Moonie's happy head. He kept putting his ears back for a scratch. Then he ran up ahead all bouncy. All I had to do was say his name and back he came. Right to me. Dog smile on his face. First time I met him.

I told Mrs. Drinker, "That is a great dog. He's welcome to come in the house and meet my grandma while I get you the money. And if I don't have enough today, I'll earn some more and I will pay you back—"

"Mason! We will not worry about the money!"

"Well, I broke your window. I should pay. And I can pay. I get money from helping people. Or maybe I can do something for you. I'm a good worker. I like work."

That's how Mrs. Drinker and I got the idea for me to take care of Moonie. She likes how it works out. Because they go to see Matt's dad a lot. He has a crazy job. He was supposed to be in Merrimack more. But he is gone. Most of the time. Seems like.

So I do that a lot now. I check on their house. Bring in the mail when they go away. I'm welcome to hang around the place. Play with Moonie. Keep him company. I do that. I love that dog.

chapter 10

BOOM

At the end of the day, I look for the boy named Calvin
Chumsky. He said he was on my bus. But I don't see
him. The bus line is not a looking-around place for me. I
look at my shoes. I shuffle forward.

The loudest kids get on our bus first. They sit at the
back. Matt Drinker. Lance Pierson. Their friends. I sit in
the middle of the bus. Face at the window. There's a lot of
talking. I like the sound being all around me. Feels like
I'm invisible, big as I am.

The bus rolls out. I think about that Dragon program.
Me, writing the sequence of mornings. I think about how
my checkpoints through town run backward on the way
home. I think this: Right before the diner is the firehouse.

I look for the bench out front. It has my best friend's name on it.

The brass plate says: *In loving memory of Benny Kilmartin.*

I've read my way through it a lot of times. Got it all memorized. It says, *Donated by Merrimack Hose Company* too. That's the name of the firehouse. So I guess they donated it to themselves. It's pretty smart. Firefighters need a place to plunk down. Me too. Sometimes I pedal Uncle Drum's old bike all the way down Swaggertown Road to town. Just so I can sit on that bench. I put my hand over Benny's name until the brass warms up.

I try to get the loving memory of Benny. It means stopping to think about him, is all. I always try for a good memory. If we can't have Benny, well, I guess I am glad the bench is there. The wood is still brown. But it'll turn to gray like the other loving memory benches in our town. You can see some of those from the bus. If you know where to look.

When Benny died, that was the *boom*. Uncle Drum said it. *Bing, bang* for Gramps and Mom. *Boom* for Benny. It just came a lot later. And maybe Benny wasn't ours. Not family. Not the same as my grandpa and my mom. But it felt like he was. To me.

Sometimes I close my eyes when the bus goes by the Merrimack Hose Company. Some days I don't want to see the bench. Some days I just know that the loving memory parts won't come. Instead I'll get stuck hurting because I don't have Benny anymore. I will get to worrying about Lieutenant Baird. The way he stops over at the crumble-down. Happens about every month. The lieutenant has questions. He is looking for answers. But he doesn't like mine.

chapter 11

LIEUTENANT BAIRD

After Merrimack Hose Company comes Merrimack Pee Dee. That's how Uncle Drum says it. Pee Dee means police department. Well, it is the station, really. There are a lot of word things that seem funny to me. This is one of them. I have heard of firehouse. But not police house. Fire station and police station. And of course we have Merrimack Hose Company. But I have not ever heard of a police company. Maybe they have that somewhere. I don't know.

Out in front of the Merrimack Pee Dee is the American flag. And a shield. Blue and gold. Painted on the door. There is a brick wall that makes an arch over the drive. Today, the number 003 cruiser is parked. Number 003 is

Lieutenant Baird. Tell you what. That's good. Means he's not at my house today.

He will come again soon. Probably. He is a person I think I could like. But we have got this problem. He still wants the same thing he wanted more than a year ago. He wants help. He wants me to remember everything that was going on the day that Benny Kilmartin died.

He even gave me that black-and-white-spotted notebook. He folded the orange pencil inside it. He said, "Now, Mason, you write it all down."

I choked. I said to him, "You don't know what you're asking."

Tell you what. That was no wisecrack.

If Lieutenant Baird had just gone over to the school they would have told him how it is with me. The reading. The writing. My troubles with that. Grandma did tell him. Uncle Drum too. He said, "Lieutenant, you should know that the kid kind of hit the *trifecta* of troubles." He said that poking his thumb at me. Then he said something about how you can see the sweating but the learning disabilities are invisible. He said, "We got major *dyslexia* here." Waggled his fingers in front of his eyes. Dyslexia is about the letters going all faded or fat.

But the lieutenant made me keep that notebook.

"Give it a try," he said. Big smile. He pushed the notebook at me like it was a big birthday gift. Thing is, it was more like a death-day gift. He gave it to me right away on the day Benny died. I remember. I let a flood of tears go right onto the cover of that thing.

Writing it down doesn't go well. But the lieutenant wants me to write *anything*. Even if it doesn't seem important. He said I can make a list of words and we will talk about them. Because that's how an investigation goes. With everyone not knowing what's important until it's all put together. Like a puzzle.

Tell you what. I have tried. But I don't think I have those pieces.

chapter 12

THE CLUSTER STOP

The loop through town is done. I missed a few check-points. Happens when I have my mind on the lieutenant. The tree fort. And Benny. There are some days I can't get away from it. I think this: I will try to tell all of that to the Dragon. Write it there. Someday.

The bus turns onto Swaggertown Road. My road. Long one. Takes you way out of the center of town.

I think about this: My mom died along this road. Hit by a car on a clear starry night. That was the *bang*. Uncle Drum said it. I was pretty little. Thought that *bang* was the sound. When the car hit her. But somewhere in these years my brain got it. *Bang* was about losing her. *Bang* was the way that hit us.

My stop is a cluster stop. It's a pretty new thing. They made it after the new developments went up. One up the hill. One down. Our house in the middle along with what's left of the orchard. The cluster stop means you can get a whole lot of kids on and off the bus at one time. Merrimack needs that now. Merrimack has been growing. That is because there is a big new plant in the city. Manufacturing. Airplane parts. So lots of workers came here. With lots of kids.

Tell you what I do. I stay ready for the stop. When I step off this bus I will hit the ground moving. Away. From Matt Drinker, Lance Pierson, and, not as much, a kid named Corey McSpirit. He's the newest one. Moved in this summer. He stands off to the side. He always wants to get down the hill to Matt's yard for a pickup game. Lacrosse. That's what they play. Kind of funny, because Matt Drinker is not a kid I'd ever give a stick to. But I have seen inside his garage. He's got a lot of those sticks.

Our house is the closest one to the cluster stop. But the bus rolls on by it for the drop. Then I have to walk back to it. Or, more like, run. Lucky I can get to our door pretty quick. And I do. Matt and Lance fire lacrosse balls at me. And you might know it. Those are *hard*. Rubber or something. They smart when they smack you. It's not as bad when they throw apples. And they can now. It is apple season.

We are halfway up Swaggertown Road. A group groan

comes from the back of the bus. Then swear words. I turn to look. Matt Drinker's phone just lost juice in the middle of a video. That's what they do back there. They lean together. Watch sports. Highlights and mess-ups.

Matt says, "We have to see that play! We have to!"

Lance tries his phone. Pokes at the screen.

Matt Drinker sees me all turned around in my seat. He says, "What are you looking at, *Butt-face*?" Tells me to turn around. I do. But then I hear him tell Lance, "Your phone is too miniature. We need a bigger screen. Where's that kid with the white hair? The one who always has his tablet? That little pygmy-sized kid."

That makes my eyes open up. Wide.

I look back again. Matt is up. He's looking over all the bus seats. Hawk for a field mouse. Then I see. Calvin Chumsky *is* on the bus after all. Two seats behind me. Must be I missed him while I was looking at my feet. He tries to sit low now. But his eyes look up. Right at me. He pushes the tablet down into his lap.

I think Calvin Chumsky should have sat up front.

Matt is up the aisle. He stands over Calvin. He points at the tablet. He says, "I need that."

Calvin says, "Well, it's mine. I don't lend it out."

Matt says, "It's just for a few minutes! Give it!" He swipes the tablet. Now Calvin Chumsky's eyes go wide. He stares at his own empty fingers.

In the back of the bus Lance Pierson tries to grab the

tablet from Matt. Matt holds it away. He mocks Calvin. Whiny voice. He says, "I don't lend it!" They laugh. Huddle up. They reach all hands in to tap on the screen.

Calvin Chumsky sits. Pushes his tongue into his cheek. Like he's got a cherry tomato in there. He rolls his eyes at me a couple of times over. I keep watch.

The bus rolls along Swaggertown Road toward our cluster stop. Corey McSpirit looks up. He says, "Hey. We're almost there, guys. Better give him back his tablet."

"Hold on, hold on," Matt says. He grips the tablet. Tilts it this way and that way. He says, "Does this thing have a camera?"

I got eyes on Calvin Chumsky. He breathes in.

Matt finds the lens. He says, "Oh good!" Then louder, he says, "Because we need a picture of Butt-hole's new STOOPID shirt. Ha ha ha!" He steps into the aisle. Aims at me. He says, "Puff up, Sweat Head. Show me your chest."

I do it. Because maybe then they'll give the tablet back.

Matt sees my shirt. The plaid tape and what Ms. Blinny wrote. That box she drew. He says, "Hey, what is that? You changed it!" He shows a snarly lip.

I say, "Yup." I give a quick look at Calvin Chumsky.

Matt cusses. Skips the picture. But he talks loud. He says, "Buttle, your brain *is* a big empty box!" The whole bus roars. I unpuff my chest.

The driver yells back. He says, "Quiet! Sit down back there!"

Then the bus rocks to a stop at the corner of Swaggertown and Orchard Drive. The air brakes hiss. Matt passes the tablet back to Calvin. Good thing.

Turns out Calvin Chumsky is getting off at our stop. Surprise to me. But tell you what. When I am busy trying to keep my sweat to myself I miss stuff. I stand in the aisle. Make myself bigger than I already am. I hold up the line to put Calvin in front of me. Best he gets off this loser cruiser before those backseaters.

On the ground, Calvin doesn't talk. He walks. Turns away like he will cross Swaggertown Road. Head up the hill. The road is named Jonagold Path. It's wrong. It was mostly Cortlands and Galas up there. The developers do not know apples. Must be Calvin lives in that upper development.

I set my sights on my house. Like always. It's about as far away as a kid can fling a lacrosse ball. Corner of my eye I see Matt and Lance run up behind Calvin. They grab him by his backpack. Dump him. He's butt on the ground. Tan-sandy shoes in the air.

A bunch of cluster-stop kids hang. Some look over their shoulders and whisper. Matt and Lance laugh. They circle around Calvin. Calvin crawls up off the pavement. Looks like a turtle getting off its back. He tells them, "Not very sporting, taking out a kid who weighs about as much as a moth." Lance steps toward Calvin.

"Yeah!" The word comes right out of my mouth. I step

forward. Chin high. I call, "Try to dump *me*! Just try!" I smile with all my teeth. Poke my chest with my thumbs to call them over. Then I stand like a post. Taller than all the rest of them. Other kids watch. Somebody says, "They're going to go after Buttle. Again."

Matt and Lance don't try to drag me down. But they jab at my knees with those lacrosse sticks. I hop out of the way. I tag Calvin. I say, "My house! Right there!" I point to the crumbledown. We run.

Calvin is not the best at this. His shoes don't help. They slap down on the gravel. I look behind us and duck a flying lacrosse ball. Then run on. I come up on Calvin's heels. I pick him up so I don't plow him down. A ball stings me in the butt. I hurry us up.

Calvin helps. Tries to keep running when his feet happen to touch on the ground. I'm swinging the heck out of him. But I can't let him go. I can't! We are up the saggy steps of the porch, Calvin and me, like we are pasted together. I take one last lacrosse ball smack in the middle of my back. Calvin is quick. He turns the knob. We fall in. Me on top of Calvin.

Crash. Groan.

I roll off him quick. Scoot my foot into the door to kick it shut. Then collapse. And breathe.

Uncle Drum in the indoor armchair says, "Hi, Mason."

Grandma leans around the kitchen corner. Looks at

Calvin and me. She says, "What's this? A heap of boys?"

I say, "Yeah. We are a heap."

She says, "Trouble at the cluster stop?"

I say, "Just some." I don't bother Grandma with that stuff.

Shayleen sticks her head out of my old room. Looks surprised to see more than just me. She gets right on it. Crabs about the noise of two boys falling into the house. Then pops away again. Cuckoo bird.

Grandma looks at tiny Calvin Chumsky. Small smile. She says, "Who wants a banana shake?"

I look at Calvin. He nods. I tell Grandma, "Two, please." Then I ask Calvin if he's okay. I ask because of that chase. And because—tell you what—if you land on a kid like Calvin, it feels like you have crushed a little pile of twigs and feathers.

Calvin nods. He is okay. Then he grins. He says, "Actually . . . that was awesome."

Uncle Drum in the armchair lets out a low laugh.

chapter 13

CALVIN IN THE
CRUMBLEDOWN

I watch Calvin. I don't think he minds about the way
it is at my house. How we have mess. Jumble of shoes
and boots and shopping bags by the door. Parts of two
broken chairs in one corner. Cobwebs in all the others.
That's the Buttles. Mess everywhere but the kitchen.
The kitchen is the one clean and shiny part of our crumbledown house.

Grandma turns her National Public Radio lower than
a whisper. She tells Calvin, "The kitchen is my domain."

Calvin looks right down at his tan-sandy shoes. Sees
that he is standing with his toes on Grandma's linoleum.
In her kitchen. He hops back. Both feet on the braid rug.
Grandma smiles. She even laughs.

Then it happens: The air above the kitchen turns thin pink—like wet raspberries. I stare at it. I know that I am the only one who sees it. But it's been a long time even for me. The pink is the color of the good parts. Best parts. Of life, I mean. Happens only sometimes. Never lasts for long. Like now, in the kitchen. Might be two seconds. I blink. Watch it fade.

And here I am thinking of two things: One is Benny Kilmartin because that's the last time I saw the pink in the air. The second thing I think about is that girl from the spelling-bee movie. How a girl like that might know about how a color could show up along with a feeling. Tell you what. I have figured out that most people do not get that. Told it to Uncle Drum once. He just closed one eye at me. Shook his head. Same for a lady at school who was giving me some tests one day. I told her I was seeing the ugly green. She told me to focus.

Calvin and I sit on the stools at the eating counter. Looks like it is for keeping people out of the kitchen. Kitchen fence. Used to be where Grandma set all the apple pies and crisps to cool. Hot from her two ovens. Sold those pies out at the stand. But that stopped and then this spot just got piled high with *Merrimack Gazette*s. Years' worth. Couldn't even sit here to eat. Until something got into Uncle Drum. Like a switch turned him on. He moved the stacks out. Did that all in one swoop. Happened pretty close after Benny died.

There is a lot that does *not* get done around here. But the newspapers, yes. Uncle Drum and Grandma look through quick. Then it's out the door and into the footwell of the truck. Off to the transfer station. I have to remind him to save me some. I stuff those in my sweaty shoes at night to dry them out. I see him sort through. Like he is picking pages. Funny thing, that is. My sweaty shoes do not care what those pages have on them.

So we sit at the kitchen fence. I make sure Calvin has the good stool. I take the one with the wobbly leg. It was me who loosened it up anyhow. Did that just by being big. And wiggly.

Grandma peels two bananas. Scoops the ice cream. Dash of vanilla. She keeps smiling at Calvin. I like to see it. Her eyes shining like minnow fish. Makes me think, there that is again. Two people liking each other right from the jump.

Then out comes Shayleen again. Right to the edge of the kitchen this time. She has colored red onto her lips.

I tell her, "This is Calvin." Then I tell Calvin, "*That* is called Shayleen."

She looks at him. From his white kitten hair down to his tan-sandy shoes. She is quiet for three whole seconds. Can't believe that.

Calvin looks back at Shayleen with her dark hair chopped so it points at her chin. She's wearing the raggedy shorts. Looks like somebody dragged those behind a car. Also, red tights. Button boots.

She blinks before she takes her eyes off Calvin. She says, "Mason. Seriously. Can we talk about how loud your body is? How *big* you sound."

I say, "I *am* big. Wrecking-ball big." Calvin laughs and I like it. Then I tell Shayleen, "There. We talked."

She says, "Do you know that I have to turn up the TV as soon as you get home?" Then she does the thing where she looks at Uncle Drum over in the armchair. Trying to stir him into this. She says, "You have heavy feet, Mason. You need to learn how to make them quiet."

I say, "I am made the way I am made, Shayleen. There is no choosing about that. Haven't we already talked about this a hundred times? And aren't you living in *my* room anyway? Shayleen? Oop! Oop! And now you're in the kitchen." I make wild eyes. Stick my arm out straight and point my finger at her button boots. Toes on the linoleum.

Tell you what. I do not do a lot of tattling. But Shayleen brings it out of me. And it is fun being fresh with her in front of Calvin Chumsky.

Grandma comes. She nudges Shayleen back to the rug. Calvin puts his hand up to his mouth. Wipes off a grin.

Shayleen bosses. She says, "And Mason, if you want to bring this little boy in—"

Grandma pushes the button on the blender. Lays

on it extra hard. Gives Shayleen thin minnow eyes. The blender is a beautiful noisy thing. There's Shayleen. Red mouth. Making words nobody can hear.

Calvin squints at her. There's not much else you can do about Shayleen. Just squint. And wonder things.

chapter 14

IN THE ROOM UPSTAIRS

We polish off the banana shakes. Grandma makes sure Calvin Chumsky tells his parents where he is. Then we go up the old tilty stairs. He is careful at climbing. Holds the rail with one hand. Brushes the old stone of the chimney with his other.

He says, "This house is awesome."

Tell you what. Calvin sees the best of this old crumbledown. He likes the chestnut beams and chisel marks. The wooden pegs. All of the parts that keep the place standing.

But the house is not the only thing he asks about. We get into the room I sleep in and Calvin whispers. Like being polite. He asks, "So, is Shayleen your sister, your cousin, or what?"

I say, "*Or what.*" That makes him laugh.

But it is not all wisecrack. It is pretty hard to explain about Shayleen.

I say, "My uncle Drum brought her home from the diner one day. Right around the end of last apple season. And I don't why he did it. But I know she is *not* his girl-friend. Just in case you wondered about that. She is too young for him."

Calvin nods. Like he knows what I am talking about.

He says, "Hmm. She's been here a long time then." He takes out his tablet. He asks me this: "So when is the end of apple season?"

I say, "Well. Not much to pick after the middle of October."

Calvin is calculating. Poking numbers on that tablet. I wait.

He says, "So, here is an estimate. If we say Shayleen got here on October fifteenth. That means she has been here three hundred thirty-six days."

I say, "Holy cow. Well. It has been long."

I dry my face on my shoulder. Doesn't work so well. I am pretty sweated up. I need a fresh shirt, is what. I wipe again. Then I see Calvin Chumsky watching me do that.

I say, "Sorry to be a gross-out. I sweat. A lot. You prob-ably saw."

Calvin shrugs. He says, "Yeah. I noticed."

I say, "It's a real thing. A problem. The doctor knows. He calls it die-ya-for—something."

Calvin says, "I think it's *diaphoresis*?"

I say, "Yeah! That's it! You know about it?"

He says, "I looked it up this afternoon." He jiggles the tablet.

I say, "Because you saw me? Saw me sweating?"

He says, "Yeah. I look up everything I encounter."

I say, "Well, then maybe you know. It is about sweat glands. Mine go overtime. Nobody knows why I got it. Might be able to get it to stop. If I can get an operation. Someday. But anyway, it is why I change my shirt at school. As long as I remember to take the extra."

Then I remember today. And I remember the shirt I am wearing. The STOOPID shirt. Except now STOOPID is covered with purple-plaid tape. I look down my chest. I remember what Ms. Blinny wrote. Comes flying right out of my mouth. I say, "Thinks outside the box." Then I say, "Ms. Blinny said that about my brain. My mind."

"It's a nice compliment," says Calvin.

"Guess so. My brain sure works different from other brains."

Calvin looks at me. Kind of has a grin on. He shrugs. He says, "Outside the box."

chapter 15

FEEDING THE DRAGON

The SWOOF is busy. Lots of kids stop in here. Some have appointments. But others just want to come. That's because of Ms. Blinny. She has a way. She cares about everyone.

I scoot on by a group. They are squeezed together at the little table by the soft couch. Making posters. Looks like. I sit down at the desk where I can talk to the Dragon. My knees bump the top. I twist to fit.

Ms. Blinny says, "Sorry. The desk is much too short for you, Mason. You are by far the tallest Dragon user."

She helps me open up my profile. But then I am all set. I remember how this works. Pretty much. But a funny thing happens. I freeze. Again.

Behind me the SWOOF is busy. Swarm of kids in here.

Ms. Blinny knows. She says, "Just go about it, Mason. Focus on the Dragon. Tell your story."

But I am thinking about a lot. Got things that knock at the front of my brain. And stuff that sticks at the back. I am trying to remember to use sequence to tell my story. I think this: Shayleen is part of my story. Whether I like that or not.

I wake the Dragon. I say this:

Well. Okay. Umm. My uncle Drum is a good guy. And that is probably why it happened. That he brought Shayleen home from the diner. Happened on a perfectly good Saturday morning. I've been waiting for her to go away ever since. Soon as Grandma saw Shayleen she pulled Uncle Drum around the corner of the kitchen. And I heard what she said to him. She's a girl, Drum. A girl.

Grandma was pretty right. Shayleen is a grown girl. She came into the crumbledown with a backpack on. Cheek full of mint candies. Drippy black eye stuff. Sniffling nose. So yeah. Grown. But Grandma meant that Shayleen was too young for my uncle Drum. And she is. And Uncle Drum told Grandma it was not like that. Shayleen was no girlfriend. He said he found her at the diner that morning. And she couldn't pay for her breakfast. So he did. She was crying. Poor thing. Poor thing. That's what he said. So then he said she needed a place to stay. Like maybe she didn't have a home. They decided to put Shayleen in my room. I was polite about her. I unmade my bed and took my sheets to the upstairs with me. I'm in the room that was my mom's room. Still looks like it is for a mom. Flowers on the wallpaper. They fixed up my bed for Shayleen. Now there she sleeps for the last three hundred thirty-six nights. Or. Wait. Umm. It could be three hundred thirty-seven now. That is an estimate. Shayleen has done the fine work of filling up my old room with a whole lot of merchandise. She gets that all from the shopping channel. Big mistake, putting her in there with the TV. Uncle Drum keeps saying we're going to move it out. Three hundred thirty-seven days. Has not happened. But I did get my own stuff out.

Anyway, umm. Oh. Yeah. Big mistake giving Shayleen the credit card too. She has bought gadgets that slice and dice. Blend and stir. She has a flying saucer thing that can keep a salad chilled and a set of stretchy bands that give you rock-hard abs. And oh yeah tubes of goo to keep your skin tan and wrinkle-free. Shayleen does not use these things much. Seems to me she just loves the buying. And opening up the boxes. She sends me out to meet the brown truck when she hears it pull up.

Tell you what. There was some fun to it at first. It was something new going on. We all got kind of stuck on watching Shayleen march across the top of the bed in her socks. Using her telephone voice. Twisting the corner of Uncle Drum's credit card in the gap between her front

-56-

teeth. Then her falling down all happy once she put her order through.

But after three hundred thirty-seven days I'm sick of fetching packages. Sick of Shayleen being bossy.

I sit back from the Dragon. I look at all the writing. It is a lot. Guess that is what it takes to feed Shayleen to the Dragon. I like the way the words look. Until they go wavy. Squash up. And slide sideways. I think this: Don't look at it, Mason. Just figure out what to say next. Write next. The sequence. But then I feel something tapping on my back. My knees bang up under the desk. I tug out of the headset and turn around.

I see the crooked smile. It is Annalissetta Yang.

chapter 16

ANNALISSETTA YANG

Tell you what. A crooked smile is not always a bad one. Annalissetta Yang, well, she is just made like that.

I met Annalissetta last year. She was new in Merrimack. So a teacher introduced her to the class. Then she wrote Annalissetta's name up on the whiteboard. I couldn't read it. But I could hear and see that her parents are very fond of letters. And if she ever wrote one of those acrostic poems from her name, well, that would be very long.

Me knowing Annalissetta kind of has to do with Benny dying. But I am the only one who knows that. Started with me staying home for one whole week after the funeral. Coming back to school after was not so good.

Seemed like there were other people besides the lieutenant who wanted to ask me questions. About Benny Kilmartin. The way I could tell this was because of the way kids stared. And whispered. And did not ask or talk about Benny at all. Stayed like that right up to the last day of fifth grade.

So then last year was the beginning of sixth grade. And there I was. Starting at the new school without my best friend. And tell you what. I missed him bad. Ms. Blinny knew that. She said to remember Benny with all my heart. She said to believe I would make new friends too. So I started saying hello to everyone in the halls. If you are looking right at someone's face you should say something. And besides, I liked it when Ms. Blinny greeted me so friendly. That all felt new. So I tried for more new. But Ms. Blinny is pretty and she doesn't sweat. And nobody had questions for her about her friend who died. So maybe she's better at it.

Anyway, I tried it. Said hello to that group of girls. The ones who seem like they are tied to each other with fishing line. They ducked chins. Bumped shoulders. They went by. Funny thing. There is always someone else coming down a school hallway. People parade. Then one day, I'm helloing and next thing I know, I'm saying hello to Matt and Lance. Matt pulled his lips inside out at me. Crossed his eyes. Lance turned backward in the hall and called out, "Hey, Buttle, if we want to hear anything out of you, we'll squeeze your head." He showed me his middle finger. Lance loves to do that.

Something about that whole thing made me miss Benny all over again. I didn't want to look at Matt and Lance so I looked down at the floor. Walked on. That's how I crashed into Annalissetta Yang. Or she crashed into me.

Annalissetta walks with a green rolling thing called a Crocodile. On four wheels. It helps her. Like for support and balance. And it works. You might not believe me when I say it, but that girl goes pretty fast with that thing. I think that was part of why we crashed. Annalissetta is a tiny girl. She went down.

I figure if you knock something over you better pick it up. Well. Big mistake. I reached down for Annalissetta's little arms. Thought maybe it would help if I got her upright again. Steady on that Crocodile. She said, "Nawuh. You can't pick me up."

I said, "Why not?"

She said, "I am capable. I can do things for myself. So if you help me when I don't need help, you underestimate me."

I said, "I do?"

She said, "Yeah. And that insults me."

I said, "Oh. Sorry." Then I wondered who told Annalissetta Yang all of that.

I stood like a stalled-out dozer. She struggled up. Tell you what. Not easy for her. Her legs keep a bend to them. Like tight muscles or something. Kids in the hall saw that. Saw me standing there. Not helping. They did not think good of me. But I knew they didn't hear her say that part about *naw-uh*, and *you insult me*.

I do not know how to do right for something like that.

Annalissetta was okay. Good thing. But when she tried to go on her way, she couldn't. That Crocodile was stuck.

She tried pushing. She said, "What the heck! What the heck!" Then she said, "Oh, I know. I have too much darn *friction*."

I saw what it was. Red knob on one wheel. Must have gotten too tight. Somehow. Knew I could put that right. So I reached. But then I stopped. I asked her, "If I fix it, would that insult you?"

She said no it would not. She smiled her funny smile. Crooked. Way up high on one side and not at all up on the other. Tiny teeth. She said, "I can't turn that thing. So, if you could, help me out. Please."

So I fixed it. Easy. And then Annalissetta thanked me. Then she took off. Rolling pretty fast. There is something to like about that.

I see her lots. She comes to the SWOOF. And now I learn this: She is a Dragon user. Helps her like it helps me. Different reason though. Her hands curl up. I know why because she told me. She said that is trouble with her muscles. That is because she has cerebral palsy.

That is a tougher trouble than my troubles. But I think this: I don't have to feel too bad for Annalissetta. That's because she does not feel bad for herself.

chapter 17

UPS

Calvin and I are drinking banana shakes. We just took another run in from the cluster stop. Good thing is, nobody took his tablet today. Bad thing is, we got some smashed apple on our shirts. Good thing is, apples don't hurt as much as lacrosse balls.

Shayleen comes out of the room that used to be mine. Cuckoo bird. She is jumping up and down. Vanilla wafer in one hand. And she is screamy. She says, "UPS! Right out front! Go, Mason! Carry it in!"

I look at Calvin. Looks like he's got a fire alarm ringing in his ear. Looks worried that there is a real fire.

I say, "It's fine, it's fine. This is what she does."

Grandma says, "We don't need more gizmos and gadgets. Oh, such waste of money." She says this to the air. Uncle Drum is the one who likes to see Shayleen all happy. He gives her the credit card. Too bad he is not around today to see her open her new box.

I slide off the stool. I tell Calvin, "Be right back."

Shayleen does not care what else is going on. If the truck comes, she wants me out there. It's always the same with her.

So here I am. Waving to the driver. That's Jerald. Been getting to know him pretty well this year. Or these 338 or 339 days. Whatever it is. I thank him. Take the box from him. It is so light I almost let it drop. I think this: Shayleen must have ordered some air.

I go into the crumbledown. Carry that box on my shoulder. I pretend it is heavy. I grunt and trip all the way into my old room.

Calvin is watching from the kitchen. Eyes wide.

I bobble that box like I'm about to drop it.

I say, "Whoopsy! Whoa!"

Shayleen yells, "You stop that, Mason! That might be something breakable!"

Might be.

Shayleen can't even remember what she has ordered.

I toss the box in the air. Catch it.

Calvin is laughing.

Shayleen says, "Mason! You faker! Not funny!" Her face is red.

Tell you what. I like this. Can't help it. Getting mad at me is the most exercise Shayleen gets in a day. So I keep it up. I jostle that box.

She says, "Set it down. On the bed. And you be respectful to me. I'm an adult! You're just a boy!"

Like that makes me some low thing in this world. I think this: With Calvin here we are *two* boys. Shayleen is outnumbered. I don't say it. But I smile about it.

I leave the box on her bed. I back out the door slowly. I get ready to fire my rhyme line at her. The one she hates.

I take a big breath. I say, "You're mean, Shayleen!"

Then I run out of my old room. Before she can chuck a vanilla wafer at me.

She eats those all day. She butters them too. Has to be the sea salt kind that comes in a tub. Uncle Drum gets it for her. She is particular.

I tell Calvin, "Sorry for that noise. Doesn't happen much at our house."

He says, "Yeah . . . Shayleen's got a loud voice all right. But the rest of you have a low hum about you. Peaceful. Kind of like a funeral home."

Then Calvin turns all red in the face. He says, "Oh, sorry. Didn't mean that as an insult."

I say, "No. It's okay. I have been to a few funerals. I think you're pretty much right."

chapter 18

A PAIR OF POEMS

In the upstairs room of the crumbledown Calvin sits on the bed tucked under the low part of the ceiling. He is on his tablet. He does a lot of that. Looking up one thing leads to looking up another.

I have a chore to do. I grab my dirty clothes up off the floor. Take them to the laundry chute in the hall. Socks. Unders. T-shirts. I come back in. Check under the bed. Sure enough, I find more.

Calvin looks up. He says, "Mason, is this room growing laundry?"

I say, "Yes. Because I am too *now and then* about it."

He says, "And where do you keep going with it?"

"The chute," I say. "End of the hall."

Then I just know it. Calvin will want to see it. He gets up and follows. He stands on his toes. Peers in. And down.

I say, "Funny thing, huh? A hole that runs through the house. Quickest way to the washer."

Calvin says, "I see that." He pokes his head into the chute. Then out. Looks at the walls around it like he's thinking about how that got built.

We stand squished together and I throw a shirt down. It catches air. Opens up on the way. Blocks the light in the chute while it falls. That square of light opens up again when the shirt hits the basket in the kitchen below. Looks like somebody is flipping a light switch.

Calvin says, "Cool." He drums his fingers in the chute. He is still looking up it and down it. He says, "This is genius. Every house should have one of these." He puts his head in there again. Calls out, "Helloooo!"

"Good-byeee!" Grandma calls back.

We laugh into the chute. Ghost voices. Then we hear Grandma laughing back. Just quiet. Like she is.

I tell Calvin, "Funny thing, I can sometimes hear her radio coming up out of the chute." Then I stuff more dirty shirts in. He watches them fall.

Calvin says, "Look at that. And it's big enough for bundles of sheets and everything. You could put *me* down that thing."

I say, "Okay. But I won't."

We hang around in the upstairs room. Kind of feels

like not much to do. Calvin shares his tablet with me. He looks up laundry chutes. Then something about house building. This is why I know that looking up one thing leads to another. But I lose attention. I am eyes out the window. I'm looking at the orchard.

I hear Calvin say, "You're not an indoor kid. Are you?"

I think. Then I say, "I guess not so much. What are you?"

He says, "I'm kind of indoor. Sorry. But my parents always try to put me outdoors."

I laugh. I tell Calvin, "Maybe it's the size of us. You fit better indoors and I fit better outdoors."

Then Calvin laughs. He says, "You want to go outside now." He says that not like a question.

He is right. I pretty much always want to be out. Thing is, there can be trouble with Matt Drinker and his friends. Even after the cluster stop. Because our yards meet up with the orchard between us. And Matt is the kind of kid who loves to stir things up. I'm used to it. But I don't want that for Calvin.

I say, "Used to have a good spot out in the orchard. A tree fort."

Calvin looks at me like he is waiting. Maybe I will say more. But all I do is look over at the two papers I have tacked up on the wall here in the upstairs room. Two poems.

Calvin looks at those too. He gets up. Taps a finger on one. The paper crackles. He says it slowly. "Hey, Mason, isn't it hard for you to read these poems?" Calvin gets that about me. Already.

I say, "Yeah. I don't read them. Not so much. Just know them by heart. They are old poems. Third grade. Brought those up from my room downstairs when Shayleen moved in. They are acrostics."

Calvin nods. He is reading.

I think this: The letters don't slide around or swell up for Calvin Chumsky. He does not think about wanting pincher eyes. And he sure doesn't need me to do it, but I say the first poem out loud anyhow.

MASON
Mammoth in size
Always with Benny
Sweaty
Only a little bit smart
Not very organized

Then I say the second poem.

BENNY
Born and adopted
Early riser
Not afraid of the dark
Not as big as Mason
Yippee

Calvin taps that last word—the *yippee*—with his finger. He grins.

I say, "Yippee. That's what Benny said. 'Yippee! I am done writing this darn acrostic poem. Time for recess!' Then he dropped his pencil on his desk and out we went."

I remember the color of that. The air turning pink all around Benny. That color floated with him when he ran to the cubbies for his hoodie. I don't tell Calvin about me seeing pink. That part is too hard to get. Even for someone smart like Calvin.

But Calvin is smiling. He says, "Yippee."

I say, "That was a pretty long time ago." Then I tell Calvin, "Don't know if you heard about him. But Benny Kilmartin is a boy from here. From Merrimack. He was my best friend. And . . . well . . . it is horrible-sad . . . but Benny is dead."

Calvin is silent.

I say, "Lieutenant Baird comes to me. Asks about what happened. Because I was there. I mean after. And before."

Calvin listens. He holds one fist in a ball under his chin.

I say, "You know something? There is a worry of mine . . ." I wipe my hands on my knees. "You should know. There has been a lot of bad luck. Around me. Like, it follows me. I think. Maybe."

Calvin says, "What do you mean? Like a curse?" He shakes his head. He says, "I don't believe in stuff like that."

chapter 19

THE NEW PART

In the SWOOF, the Dragon computer is free. I find Ms. Blinny. She is on tiptoe. Roll of masking tape clamped in her teeth. She is trying to flatten a new poster to the wall. The poster wants to curl up. She uses both elbows, one shoulder. She tears a strip of tape. It floats back into her hair. Sticks. She says, "Mmm . . . mmm . . . mmaw!" Then she says, "Oh! Dropped the tape!" She leans out to watch it roll over my foot. Then . . . *pop*! The poster snaps up like a window shade. Hits her in the nose.

Her eyes close tight. Then she laughs a big laugh.

I dry my sweaty hands. Pick up the tape and help Ms. Blinny. We get that poster on the wall right. She says, "Here's to teamwork!" She shakes my hand. Ms. Blinny does not seem to mind my sweat. Neither does Matt Drinker's dog, Moonie. He kind of likes sweat.

I ask Ms. Blinny, "Is it okay if I talk now? I mean write? If I talk out my writing? Or write out my talking? On the Dragon?"

She says, "Yep. Clear schedule."

I have figured out the best way for me to talk to the Dragon. I take two tissues. Tuck one under each earphone so I don't sweat those up. Then I stack my fists into two potatoes on the desk in front of me. I rest my forehead on them. Helps me to shut off from the rest of the SWOOF. I can guess that I am a strange thing to see. Mammoth kid. Face on the desk. Talking away. Tissue ears. But the SWOOF is a safe place. Say something to tease somebody and Ms. Blinny will send you out.

Today I get a slow start. But then I tell this to the Dragon:

Okay umm well. I have been waiting to say it. But there is a new part of my story now. And that is Calvin Chumsky. He has come over to my house. I mean inside the crumbledown. Three days now. We are friends. Heard him say it to his parents.

So the way we got to be friends is this. Calvin came to my house. The first day was all by accident. Because of some chasing. The second day was not as much by accident. But still because of chasing. The third day well he came over on purpose. That was a day the lacrosse kids stayed to use the school field. Backseats of the bus were empty. So. All quiet at the cluster stop. And Calvin walked home with me anyway. He just wanted to. With me.

The earphone pops off my one ear. Makes me jump out of my sweaty skin. I look behind me. There she is again. Annalissetta Yang.

She says, "Hi. What are you writing today, Mason?" She pats one of her backward hands on my shoulder. Holds on to the Crocodile with her other. She says, "Looks like it's going great on the Dragon, huh, Mason? Look at all your writing!" She swirls one arm.

I nod. I see a tissue waving by my eye. It is still stuck on the side of my head. I peel it off. Use it to mop up.

I tell Annalissetta, "Works pretty well for me. Talking to the Dragon. This kind of writing. Sorts it out for me. I guess I do have a story to—"

Annalissetta laughs out loud. Points at the computer screen. She says, "Mason, you're still typing!"

I say, "Darn!" Then that word goes up on the screen. Big letter D there. I tell the Dragon to stop listening. Push the headset away from me. Annalissetta tilts her chin up. She has a sort of *puh-huh-huh-huh* kind of laugh. She gets that going. She is on and on about that.

Ms. Blinny looks up from her desk. She says, "Hey there, Annalissetta." She smiles with her big teeth.

Annalissetta shows little teeth back at her. The crooked smile. Ms. Blinny says, "How about you give Mason some space while he's at the Dragon?" Ms. Blinny closes one eye at Annalissetta like she is saying, *You already know this*.

Annalissetta makes a circle mouth. She says, "Oh, oh, oh! Sure! Sorry I interrupted you, Mason." She gives me another pat on the back. Then she shakes her hand. She says, "Boy! You sure are a sweater!"

I think this: Better I am a sweater than a gross-out. Funny thing how Annalissetta Yang just says what she says. She won't waste time at finding words that are not the ones she is thinking. She uses the ones that come right up front.

Ms. Blinny says, "Annalissetta, you're welcome to come back for the Dragon later. You have fifth period free, right? Will that work?"

Annalissetta says, "Yep! Okay. I get it. Privacy, privacy, privacy." She rocks her head while she says it. Then she cranks the Crocodile around and heads out the door. Then I can't see her. But my brain makes a picture. She is scooting down the hall. Pretty fast. Tell you what. My brain is probably right about that.

chapter 20

APPLESAUCE

The apple hits the side of the crumbledown. Bursts into pieces. Two more come. I holler to Calvin, "Duck! Run!" And there we go skittering close beside the house. This is how it goes. Every day except weekends and Wednesdays, when there is after-school lacrosse. I'm sick of it. Calvin too. The next apple loops in. Another rides the wind by our ears.

Calvin says, *"Aerodynamic apples!* Who knew?"

Tell you what. Matt Drinker and Lance Pierson do not get tired of it. Calvin says it is because they have two targets now. I think this: Two targets *again*. I remember. They used to get at Benny and me up in the tree fort. Get us stuck up there like a couple of pigeons.

Calvin and I run. Dash around the corner. Get onto the front porch. We crouch low behind the old stuffed armchair. Calvin fits. Me, not so much. I hug my knees.

I hear Matt Drinker calling, "Oh, Butt-head! Got some applesauce-y for ya! Come and get it!" Then he says, "You too, Fetus-face!"

Calvin rolls his eyes at me. Not so fond of the nickname. He stands up and hollers, "Meathead Matty!" He ducks down again. Tucks both fists under his chin while more apples rain in. Calvin tells me, "I love this fat chair. Nice fortress."

I tell him, "Used to be indoors. Saw a mouse come out of the stuffing one day. Uncle Drum had me move it out here."

We wait. No apples flying. I stick my head out for a look. No Matt. No Lance. But there is Corey McSpirit. Coming up the hill. He looks all around. He calls out, "Matt! Lance! Hey, are we going to play? Come on! Guys?" He pops a lacrosse ball straight up in the air. Traps it back in the basket of his stick. Swishes left and right. Then don't you know, Matt's dog, Moonie, comes up behind Corey. Tail wagging. Body wiggling. Nose sniffing.

Corey calls again, "Hey! Guys! Where are you?" I wonder the same thing.

Calvin pokes one finger into a hole in the chair cover. He whispers, "Here, mousey, mousey." No mouse comes.

But Moonie does. He bounds onto the porch. Into the

chair. He bounces in circles. Blur of black and white. He leaps over the back. Finds me. Calvin too.

Calvin says, "Uh-oh."

I pop up tall. Big shower of apples slam the porch. I see Matt and Lance behind the trees. Reloading. Three at a time. They swing back to fire again. Matt will shoot right where his own dog is standing. It's how he is. Apples spatter across the deck boards. Moonie jumps and twists. He would catch the apples. Eat the pieces. But they are coming in too hard. Too fast. Poor dog. He ducks behind my legs.

I say, "This is it, Calvin! We gotta get inside! Dog too!" I holler, "Go!"

Calvin moves. Slips his skinny self out from behind the chair. His shoes slap down on the old porch planks. He dives on the doorknob and turns it. He is in. Then Moonie. Then me.

I hear Matt Drinker holler, "Hey! That's *my* dog, Buttle!"

I slam the door.

Moonie turns himself round and round on the old carpet inside the crumbledown. He stops on his elbows. Wags. Shows eye whites. He circles again. Makes us laugh. Best dog ever.

Shayleen marches out of the room that used to be my room. Goes right to the door. Same one I just slammed. She hauls it open. She steps onto the porch and screams,

"That's right! Beat it, you little jerks! Beat it!" Then I know Matt and Lance and Corey must be running away. Then, even louder, Shayleen roars, "Quit disturbing the *peace!*"

She slams the door hard. Harder than I did. Moonie freezes. One paw held in the air. Looks at Shayleen. She hops on one foot. Kicks apple chunks off her boot. Stamps her feet. She says, "Mason, *do not* bring those bad boys to the door like that! My window is right there!"

I say, "You think I asked them to come, Shayleen?"

Calvin says, "You sent engraved invitations as I recall." He looks at Shayleen. "He *didn't*. You do understand that, right?"

I say, "Yeah, I even told them to aim where Shayleen is. She loves smashed apples, is what I said."

Uncle Drum laughs in the indoor armchair. Just quiet.

Shayleen keeps crabbing. She says, "By the way, I tried to open that window to speak to them. But it's stuck. *Again.*" She gives Uncle Drum the stink eye. Like that will make him fix it. He's sitting way deep in the soft chair. But he hangs his arm over the side. Clicks his fingers to call Moonie over for a pat. Shayleen huffs. She says, "I'm only asking for a little fresh air."

I say, "The fresh air is outside, Shayleen." It is no wise-crack. True thing. I say, "Trouble is, you are always in the house. Except for just now when you went out there to holler."

Shayleen says, "Speaking of *in the house* . . . I see you let that *rambunctious* dog in again."

I say, "Yeah. Well. You got eyes then."

She says, "Drum! Do you hear what he's saying to me?"

My uncle doesn't blink. He rubs Moonie's ears.

Shayleen grunts. "Ugh!" She stomps away. Back to the room that used to be mine.

Moonie scarfs up the apple pieces Shayleen brought in on her feet. He is the kind of dog who eats like he hasn't seen food for days. And will never see any again. But I know he's got a whole good bin full of kibble at his own house. Yellow dog chips for snacks too.

I know I should take him home. I will not just put him outside because tell you what. Swaggertown Road is right out front and that's not a safe place for dogs. I figure he can stay awhile. He has before.

I clap once. I say, "Come on, boy!"

He heads up the stairs. Turns around at the top and sits. He waits for Calvin and me. Tail wagging so hard it swats the dust up off the floor. I laugh. I tell Calvin, "Look at that dog. Broom for the Buttle house."

chapter 21

BRAMBLES AND LOPPERS

So the good part is Calvin is here and Moonie is too. The bad part is we are kind of stuck in the room upstairs again.

Calvin pokes around on his tablet. I sit by the window with my arm around Moonie Drinker. Scratch him under the chin. When I stop he bumps my hand for more. Love that.

Calvin calls the upstairs room our *vantage point*. From the window we can see into the Drinkers' yard. It is the way the shape of the land works. We are high up. It's a double hill. First is the short hill. Kind of grows off the back of the crumbledown. Right close at the back of our house.

This window looks down on that. Mess of brambles and thorns because Uncle Drum quit mowing it years ago. Next is the long hill. Where I rode the sled across the rows of apple trees and into the Drinkers' basement that time.

Calvin says, "Are they playing yet?" Sometimes he doesn't look up from the tablet.

I check the yard. I say, "Won't be long. They have Corey McSpirit today. He always gets it going."

Calvin says, "Yeah. Lacrosse is probably his favorite thing about Matt and Lance. Corey is in it for the game."

That's all we are waiting for. When they get a good game going down there, they don't care a crumb about chasing Calvin and me.

I watch and wait. I do some thinking about the old tree fort. I have an ache to be making a plan and hammering on boards again. Like I did with Benny. We made our own place to be. Outside. Sky and leaves over our heads.

Well, I saw that the yellow police tape is down. Finally. Maybe Lieutenant Baird would say I could go back there now. But not so sure I want to. Truth is, I stood pretty close one day. Looking at the place where the ladder used to be. And then at the grass below. It was the lieutenant who took the ladder away. Back when Benny died. He told me it is part of his puzzle. Something about the way the rung snapped. Gets me in the gut. Because I just think this: Missing ladder. Missing Benny.

Sometimes I think it: I could build another one. Start new. But it puts a fly in my head thinking that I could do something wrong. Build a bad ladder again. And I am not so sure Calvin would like a tree house. Been in the orchard with him plenty. I pull myself up into the trees. Just some. But Calvin stays below. He doesn't say. But I know. He is not a climber.

I look out down the hill. I nudge Calvin. I say, "Lacrosse game! They're playing. Come on."

Calvin packs up the tablet. I clap for Moonie to follow.

We are out the door heading to the back of the crumbledown.

There is a pretty good spot to be. Right between the short hill and the long hill. Calvin calls it the dip. And it is one. Low spot. Close behind our house.

We get down there. Got Moonie hopping around. Running little circles and looking for something to pick up in his mouth. He finds an apple. Drops it at my feet. I roll it like a bowling ball. He chases.

The whole time Calvin faces the short hill. Right close at the back of the crumbledown. He likes to measure things with his eyes. I know he is thinking something.

He says, "Hey, Mason, what's with the way the hill is cut there? How come it drops off so flat? Like a wall? And what's behind the brambles?"

That is a lot of questions. I try to think what to answer. It is a bit mixed up in my brain.

Calvin knows. He says, "Oh, sorry. Just wondering out loud."

He steps up to the wall of thorns and brambles. He is curious about it. Same way he is for chimneys and laundry chutes. He studies it up with his eyes. Moonie comes back with the apple. Drops it. He stands beside Calvin. Sniffs along the ground. He picks up a paw. He scratches at the hill.

I look at Calvin. Calvin looks at me. Then Calvin sticks his skinny hand right in there behind the thorns. He is careful about it. I hear taps. A sound like wood under Calvin's little knuckles. Then a rattle. Like metal.

He says, "Whoa! This is a door, Mason! I just found a latch!"

I say, "Holy cow!" I turn to run.

Calvin calls, "Wait! Where are you going?"

I call back. I say, "Going to get the loppers! Cut the thorns! So we can get in there!"

All the way to the shed, I hope like heck I can find them. Trouble is our shed is a mess. But good luck comes. I do find the loppers. Hanging up. Little bit rusty. But I think they will still cut.

When I get back Calvin is grinning. He says, "Mason. I have an idea."

He wants me to cut through the brambles all around the door edge. Side and top. But not the side with the hinges on it.

He says, "When we open the door it will be like a blanket of thorns swinging with it."

I say, "Camouflage!"

Calvin nods his big nod. "Nobody will ever know."

I like this idea. I hold my elbows high. I stick the tip of the loppers into the pricker canes. Cut along like I am using giant scissors. Tell you what. Tougher than I thought. The canes are thick. The loppers are lousy. Keep getting them stuck.

Calvin tells me how great I am doing. But all I think is this: Wrong tool for the job. I stop to wipe sweat. Then go at it again. I turn the loppers this way. That way. Tell you what. This is giving me blisters.

I try to think what would work better. Pruners. Maybe. We have an orchard. So we sure have pruners. Somewhere. But even if I find them, it will be tons of snipping. Bare hands in the thorns. One cane at a time. We will be forever, and Calvin has to be home before dark. In time for supper. That is the rule.

And then I think of it. I have a handsaw! My own. Uncle Drum bought that for me on my tenth birthday. Right before Benny and I started to build the tree house. And I sure used it plenty. But there is trouble about that handsaw. Last I looked for it, I was trying to help the lieutenant with his puzzle. I couldn't find it. Not anywhere. And now I can't think when I had that last. And maybe it wouldn't be any better for this job. Might snag on the canes. But don't you know it, I can't get that out of my head.

So here I go again. Up to the shed. Calvin comes with me. Moonie Drinker too. We search. High and low. Up and down the workbench two times over. Then I pull out the rakes and shovels. Flowerpots and rusty tomato cages. Moonie puts his nose in every corner. Tail wagging now and then. Like he has found a new friend in every spider web. Calvin and I laugh. But we do not find that handsaw.

I tell Calvin, "Stuff goes missing, is all. That's how it is around my house."

So we head back to the dip in the hills. I see that the sun is sinking. I pick up the hand-eating loppers again. Set to work. Calvin is the lookout. Goes to the spot where he can see down to the Drinkers' yard. Moonie has a lie-down in the grass. He doesn't go far from me.

It's not long before Calvin comes back. Running in those tan-sandy shoes. He says, "That's it! The game is breaking up, Mason. And I have to get home."

I say, "But I almost got this!" I clamp the loppers down on the canes. I stay at it. I want to pull on that door so bad!

Calvin gives me about one more minute. Then he

says, "You really better stop. What if they come looking for Moonie?" And don't you know the dog looks up when he hears his name. Head on a tilt.

I say, "Darn!" I drop the loppers. I turn around to look at Calvin and there I see Matt Drinker. Standing right behind my new best friend.

I walk forward, is what I do. Big long strides.

Calvin looks confused. But then he makes huge eyes like he knows. And both of us wonder this: What has Matt Drinker seen?

Matt has Moonie's leash. Twirls that in one hand. The dog stands up. Wags a tiny wag. Licks his lips. He walks around behind my legs. Sits.

I say, "Hey, Matt. Hi." He gives me a plain face back. Not that mean. But not that nice.

He says, "I came to get my dog."

I say, "Oh. Right. Well, I was about to bring him down to you."

That is a true thing. If Moonie comes over I take him back to the Drinkers' always around suppertime.

I say, "But we were . . . just finishing up this . . . chore. Down here. Had a chore. For my uncle Drum."

That is a not-true thing. Calvin gives me a sly eye.

Funny thing. It is all lost on Matt. He just reaches around me. Clips Moonie to the leash.

And then . . . then . . . the part I hate. He yanks him and hauls him. And I know, because I have seen, he will do that to the dog all the way home. Doesn't need to. But he does.

I say it to Calvin. I say, "I wish he wouldn't do that. I know he doesn't mean anything by it. But man, I do not like that."

Calvin is giving me a funny look. Like I must have that wrong.

But he doesn't say, and it's time for him to go. And we are glad we are not caught trying to open a secret door.

I say, "Tomorrow. Tomorrow we get through and we open that door."

Calvin shows me a thumbs-up.

chapter 22

PERMISSION TO ENTER

Tell you what. I wash up for my supper and all I can do is think about that door.

At the supper table I say, "Hey, found a door in the hill. Out back of the house." I jab my thumb to point so they know where I am talking about.

Shayleen yells, "Mason! You almost stabbed me with your fork!"

She is right. I forgot to put that down.

"The root cellar," Uncle Drum says. "Hmm. Empty."

Grandma says, "That hasn't been used since the 1960s. I was a girl. They used to pack it with jars of peaches and pickles. Pumpkins and squashes. Bags of carrots and turnips."

I say, "Yeah?"

Grandma nods. I like when she remembers old times. Old things about the crumbledown and the Buttle farm.

I say, "Can I go in there?"

Uncle Drum says, "If you can get it open." He says it like he thinks I won't. Not to be mean. It's just what he thinks.

Shayleen sits there shaking her head. Like she knows anything.

I say, "But if I do?"

Grandma and Uncle Drum say what they usually say. "Suit yourself. Stay out of trouble."

I nod my head and think. Staying out of trouble is pretty much what Calvin and I have in mind. We want to ditch the apple throwers.

Shayleen knocks me out of the thought. She pushes the roll of paper towels at me. She says, "Wipe down! We're eating dinner, Mason! Ugh!"

I think this: We could be away from Shayleen too.

I am giving her a look when the phone rings. Her eyes cross. I get that. The ringer is so loud it could shake the plaster off the walls. Good thing we don't get a lot of calls.

I pick up and guess what? It is Matt Drinker. Calling for me. You wouldn't think this would happen. But it does.

He says, "Mason." Because this is when he calls me Mason instead of something with *butt* in it. He says, "My mom wants you to come over tonight. For Moonie. She's going out for a meeting."

I say, "And you'll be there?"

He says, "Yeah. But I'm busy. So you should come for Moonie. Be the dog-sitter. My mom will pay."

I know what this is. I know because Moonie does not need a dog-sitter when someone is home. This is Matt Drinker being scared to be alone. Funny thing, the way he is. Like two different Matts in one dude. I will go down there and he will not be the apple-flinger, lacrosse-ball-stinger kid. He won't whack me with a stick. And he won't say much at all. He will play video games. He will tell me to have as many snacks as I want from the Drinkers' pantry. Same place the yellow dog chips are. He will sit in the low game chair. Punch the buttons on his controller. He will pretty much ignore me. But Moonie won't.

I finish supper and help clear. Then I go. I go a little bit for Matt's mom. A little bit for the money. But mostly, I go to be with Moonie.

On my way down the hill I stop. I turn back to look at the wall of brambles. I think about that door in the hill. And the root cellar behind it. Try to imagine it in my brain.

I cannot wait to get in there.

chapter 23

THE DOOR SWINGS

Calvin and I are ignoring some rain.

I grunt. I say, "We are going to get through this door!"

He says, "This is a *beast*!" He tugs with me. Backpack swinging.

He is right. The door in the hill is as stuck as a thing ever was. The brambles are cut. We hold them back with a stick. We fiddle with the latch. It wiggles and jingles but is worthless to pull on. Not much to grip, and it is damp from rain. We both try. Our fingers slide off.

I say, "There must have been a handle. Once. Something to pull."

Calvin nods like he agrees.

I get ahold of the edge of the door. Pry my fingers in deep. I pull it. Something gives. Little bit. I dig in again. Bend back two of my fingernails while I am at it. Don't care.

I tug. And I say it again. "We will—ugh!—get this open! We will!"

And then it gives! I stumble back. Nearly knock Calvin over. I grab him. Keep him on his feet. The wood door swings. The hinge sings an old whiny note.

We stand squished at the door. We look. But we don't go in. All we can see is the dark of it. Calvin and I don't speak. We blink our eyes. I think about my great- and great-great-grandparents and all those early Buttles. Wonder how they could see to find their pickle jars and pumpkins.

Calvin says, "We are going to need some light."

I go fast. Up to the house. I fetch Uncle Drum's flashlight off the nail by the door. I run back. Kind of go slipping as I run round the porch and come down the short slope. It is slick from the rain.

I shine the light inside. I take two steps down to the packed dirt floor. Calvin follows. I hold up the light. Bring it slow along the inside. Along the stony walls.

Calvin whispers. He says, "Whoa-ho. Wow-how."

Turns out you don't say much more than that. Not when you just opened up a place nobody has been in since a grandma was a girl. You just stand in your sweaty shoes and blink a lot. Think about bushels and jars. And all of that. And you follow the flashlight sweeping along those walls. And you wait for your eyes to adjust. Because you want to see more.

The walls are made of stones. With old mortar between them. And some packed dirt. Maybe. Hard to say. I pick it with a fingernail. What I have left of that. Some of the stuff makes crumbs. Some holds tight. The ceiling is low. Made of wood. I take a step. Don't you know, I bang my head. "Ow!"

Calvin says, "Oh, Mason! Keep low!"

I look up to see the beam I walked my head into. Dirt falls in my eyes so I blink that out. Wipe sweat down my face. I tell Calvin, "Well, I guess I won't forget that now." I rub the spot. Feel an egg coming up there. Not too bad.

I think this: The root cellar is a room. Not so big. About like if you put a few good closets together.

We step over old boards. Shine the flashlight along the walls and into a few *recesses*. *Recesses* is what Calvin calls them. We walk to the back wall.

Calvin pats it with both hands. He says, "This wall is the foundation of your house. See? And then they built two side walls and capped them so it wouldn't collapse . . ."

He is looking all up and down the space while he talks.

I hold the flashlight in one hand. Dry the other on my pants. I brush my fingers along the stony, stony walls. I am thinking. Remembering a story I heard. When Calvin is quiet I ask him, "You ever heard of the Caves of Lass-Co?"

"Caves?" Calvin shakes his head no.

I say, "There is a true story. I heard it on the radio. National Public Radio. You know. It's what my grandma listens to all day. It's news and music and stories. Well, there is guy named Garrison Keillor. That's her favorite one. He does a talking bit on there. And he told the story about the caves."

Calvin says, "Caves? In a place called Lass-Co?" He reaches into his backpack.

I say, "Yeah. Lass-Co in France. France over in Europe."

"Oh . . . France . . ." Then that part seems interesting to Calvin.

I say, "Bet you could find it. On your tablet."

Next thing I see is his face all lit up. The tablet is shining up at him. He is clicking around. Few seconds more and he is looking super close at some pictures.

I say, "Did you find it? Did you find something about Lass-Co?"

Calvin Chumsky is silent. Face in that tablet. He is nodding his big nod. He looks up and all around the root cellar. One full sweep.

He tells me, "Mason. This is going to be perfect."

chapter 24

FRENCH LESSON

I set a sack of apples on Ms. Blinny's desk. She opens the top and peeks in. She says, "From your place, Mason? From your orchard?" She looks at me. Big smile. She reaches for an apple and the whole bag tips. One runaway. Ms. Blinny makes the save. She holds the apple in her two hands. She says, "Look at it! What perfection! Thank you, Mason. I shall treasure these gifts." She pretends to hug the sack of apples. Then she says, "I meant to ask, did your family open the apple stand this season?"

I tell her no. Wish I could say yes. I think it plenty: There is still good left of our place. We have acres of healthy trees.

I tell Ms. Blinny, "Anytime you want more apples, just

tell me. Good ones keep coming. We have varieties. Trees keep making fruit. No matter what."

Then I get myself settled at the Dragon. Tuck my tissues in under the earphones. I look at my fingernails. Chipped up from prying on that root cellar door. Well worth it, is what that is. I lean my head down and tell this to the Dragon:

So I told Calvin a true story. One I know because Garrison Keillor told it. He is my grandma's favorite. On the radio. Tell you what even that tiny jingle the vegetable peeler makes is too loud for when Mr. Keillor is on. Grandma stops real still when she listens to him. Me too.

Best thing is when I catch Mr. Keillor two times in one day. Double chance to stick the story in my head. And that's what happened. I heard Mr. Keillor say there are paintings on a wall in a cave. In France. In Europe. A place called Lass-Co. Except now Calvin showed me that French people put an X on the end of some words. I can try to memorize how to spell Lascaux. I think this Dragon knows how. But umm I don't think I will take French.

Okay. But anyway. Garrison Keillor said it was four big boys. Just outside playing around that found those paintings on the inside of the caves. Pictures of animals and stick people. It is all primitive art is what Calvin said. Means super old. Might have been there seventeen thousand years with nobody knowing it. Maybe more.

Tell you what. That is old. It is older than apples. Those boys also had a dog with them. Dog called Robot. I have a picture of their dog. In my mind. Looks just like Matt Drinker's dog, Moonie. Black spots on white. My brain chooses that because Moonie is my favorite dog. Umm. So. Calvin found a whole Caves of Lascaux tour on his tablet. That is the only way to see it now. We have sure been looking at it a lot. Used to be they let people in the caves. But then all that human breath was bad for the paintings. Mr. Keillor said so. And Calvin read that to me too. But what we saw on the tablet was all that old art. Tell you what. That was amazing.

chapter 25

INSIDE BISHELL'S HARDWARE

Saturday morning I ride Uncle Drum's bike downtown to Bishell's Hardware. Long way. But I like what I am going for. Makes the pedaling easy. I pick out two whisk brooms. A pack of fresh batteries for Uncle Drum's flashlight. I take those up to the cash register. I look to my left. I see the blue of old blue jeans. Standing right beside me is one of Benny Kilmartin's dads. It's Andy. The most at-home dad. The dad I know the best.

Feels so good to see him—I breathe in. I say, "Andy! Hi!" Comes out like a shout. Too much in this early morning quiet of Bishell's Hardware.

I look down the aisle behind me. I see leaf rakes. Bags of birdseed. Work gloves waving from a go-round rack.

Tell you what. I think I'm going to see Benny. Coming up to the register with something cool in his hands. Might be a metal tie-down or a pulley. Benny loves hardware stuff. Anything from the racks and spools and the tiny drawers at Bishell's.

Then I see Andy's face. Looking back at me. Like he's been punched. And I remember. There was a funeral. There is a loving memory bench.

Boom.

Sometimes I cannot keep my head around it. That Benny died and then stayed gone.

I stand in the time-freeze in Bishell's. Thinking.

My brain starts running memories. I think about the Kilmartin house. It was always getting built up instead of crumbling down. All because of Andy. He did their roof over. Patched up ours too. That time we had the snow come in. He built bookshelves for Benny's other dad, Franklin. He made a bottle tree. From rebar and empty wine bottles. The sun came through the colored glass. Greens and yellows spilling all over Benny's shirt. His arms. Andy grilled us strip steaks and peaches that same day. He showed us how a rock wall goes together. Benny and I helped him build the one at the bottom of their driveway. Solid. Like a root cellar. One time Benny went to bed with a fever. I stayed to paint window trim with Andy. That's when he taught me the right way to load a paintbrush.

I blink.

Paintbrushes. That's what Andy has on the counter at Bishell's Hardware. He set them there the same second I set down the batteries and whisk brooms.

But Andy has his head down. Stone still. I see his plaid shirt. It breathes. Then it is like he grows thinner inside of it. Then he walks out of the hardware. Leaves the brushes on the counter.

Two clerks watch him go out. Then one looks at me. Like he thinks he knows my story. Sad to see you. He swallows. Rings me up.

I take my bag. Go look for Andy on the street. But he is gone. I sit on the loving memory bench out front of the hardware. Just for a minute. Put my hand over that brass plate. I know what it says. Because this one is for my gramps. Grandma told me he came downtown to Bishell's every weekend. Always needed something or other. So the bench has the name Buttle on it. Like Mom's. It is a tough thing. None of these ones who are gone was very old. Least old was Benny.

Before I ruin this morning all the way, I go. I strap the bag with the whisk brooms and the batteries onto the back of Uncle Drum's old bike. Pedal out of town. I start that long ride out Swaggertown Road. Legs pumping.

I think it: Calvin will be waiting. We have got something cooking and I can't wait to start.

chapter 26

THE CHUMSKY PARENTS

Calvin and I do a whole day of cleaning up the root cellar. We drag out the old boards. We sweep and then resweep with our whisk brooms. I work high. He works low. We make sure no one is around. No one looking up from Matt Drinker's yard. We sweep a pile of crud out the door.

Some spots are cleaned right down to stone. Calvin calls them *recesses*. Then he talks about *chambers*. Chambers is what his tablet says about the parts of the Caves of Lascaux.

We find one hole in the door. Pinkie finger–sized. Like mine. Not Calvin's. He has a smart idea. We get a piece of rope and push it through. We tie knots in both ends. One inside the cellar. One out. Calvin says, "We can just yank on it. All the quicker to close it." That's the last thing we do for the day.

The sky has the color of just before dark. We go up and find Calvin's mom and dad on the porch of the crumbledown. Just arrived. Two bags of groceries in their arms.

They tell Grandma, "Nice to meet you." They say, "We thought you should know. He does have parents."

Calvin snorts a laugh about this.

His dad says, "Just so you know, Mason is welcome at our house too. We have a helper there to *supervise* after school. An adult. Of course, Calvin tells us he's having more fun here. I can imagine. Your orchard lands are beautiful." He sweeps a hand backward. He says, "This is just what we hoped for when we moved here. Thank you for letting Calvin play in all your acres."

I wonder if Calvin's parents know about the chasing. And maybe the part about how we don't get *supervised* all that much here. I wonder.

His mom says, "You've been so nice to host him. We felt we should contribute. He must be eating you out of house and home."

I say, "Are you kidding? Calvin? He fills right up. There's not much to him." Then I guess they already know this.

They laugh. Bring the bags inside.

Shayleen comes out of the room that used to be my room. I bet she heard the grocery bags crackling. A shopping noise. Top of the bag I see bananas and vanilla wafers.

The Chumsky parents talk to Grandma. I keep half my ear on it. They want to make this official. I don't know what that is about. Not until Grandma says, "No. I won't take a penny. He's a friend. He's always welcome here."

Then I get it. She does not want us to be Calvin's babysitters. That's good. Seventh-grade dudes do not need babysitters.

The Chumsky parents say, "Well, at least accept the groceries. It's just a few snacks. Please."

Grandma tells them, "Just this once."

I ask Calvin does he want to wash up before he goes home. There is dirt under his fingernails. All over his tiny paw hands. He says, "No. My parents love it when I get dirty."

His mom says, "We do!"

Calvin says, "They just don't want to be there while it's happening."

His dad says, "True."

His mom says, "True."

They all laugh. Calvin grinds his gritty knuckles in his ear.

I say, "We have plenty of dirt here."

Then the three Chumskys go up the hill. Up Jonagold Path.

Tell you what. I was sorry when Uncle Drum sold that off. Sorry we lost so many Galas and Cortlands to the bulldozers. But I am not sorry we got the Chumskys living up there now. Not one bit.

chapter 27

SEEKING A TUBE

Next few days wc brave it. We go down to the construction sites. Creep along the yards. Watch out for the
apple chuckers. We come back with two five-gallon buckets. Little bit cracked. Picked those from the dumpsters.
We don't need any trouble about trespassing or stealing.

We turn the buckets upside down inside the root cellar. They are something to sit on.

So we have our place. It is away from Shayleen. Away
from speeding lacrosse balls and apples and swatting
sticks. We sit. I don't say it, but I think about the tree fort.
The leaves. The limbs. The breezes. Miss those in the
root cellar. I liked the work of getting in here. Sweeping

it down was fun. But there is not so much to do. And it's still pretty dark.

Don't you know, that's when Calvin says, "Mason, I have an idea."

He brings up a picture on his tablet. Shows me a tube stuck into the ceiling of a house. Looks like there is a light on inside it.

He says, "Do you get it? It's a light shaft. It collects light at the top from outdoors and brings it all the way into the room below."

I say, "What? How?" Then I say, "You want to put one of those in here?"

He says, "Yes. We can make one." He points up over our heads. He says, "We'll put it right through there." I look up at the old boards and wonder about the whole thing. Calvin says, "I've been thinking about this. A lot. I know how to approach it. We're going to need some parts. And I think I know where to get them."

I say, "Where? The construction sites?"

Calvin Chumsky nods his white head.

So we go and we search around the dumpsters some more. Calvin holds up a piece of plastic pipe like they use for plumbing.

"We need something like this," he says. "Only bigger." He makes a wide circle with his arms. Like he is hugging someone round and invisible.

I say, "I don't know a reason for plumbing pipes to be that big. What you're showing me is way bigger than the flushing hole of a toilet, Calvin."

Calvin asks me, "But have you seen if any of these new houses have raised decks or screen porches?"

"Yeah. Sure. Number fourteen and eighteen. Crispin Drive."

"Does anybody live there?"

I say, "Not yet."

Calvin says, "Good. Dumpster time!"

Turns out Calvin is after one of those big cardboard tubes. The kind for making a column of concrete. Like what the porches and decks sit on.

So we check dumpsters. We crawl below the porches at numbers fourteen and eighteen Crispin Drive. No luck. We walk through two new sites on McIntosh Circle on the way home. That's where we see something. Calvin and I run straight to it. There are words on the side. Calvin reads it: *Sonotube form*. But it has been sliced open. Calvin says, "Close. But that won't do." He says, "It's not long enough anyway."

He says, "If I calculated right, we need about six feet."

I say, "Six whole feet?" I make big eyes at him. "What! That's more than me! I can't see us having any luck finding that."

Almost as soon as I say those words, we do have luck.

Right close to home. We are two doors down from Matt Drinker's house and we see a new foundation is in. Six cement columns stick up from the ground like they are waiting for something to land on them. Calvin and I sort through a lot of torn-up Sonotube *remains*.

Remains. That's what Calvin calls the fat curls of cardboard. And then one—just one—nice long tube. It is the fattest of all. And it is whole.

We lift it. It is not heavy, but it is awkward. Part of that is because Calvin is at one end and I am at the other. One short. One tall. This is not so good for balance. We got some swing and stumble going here. Truth is, I could put this tube on my shoulder with Calvin inside of it and make the climb home just as fast. But the way I feel about it is this: The tube is Calvin's find. It is his prize. And there is great glory in carrying home a prize. But it is too long and rolly for Calvin to manage alone. He needs my help.

So here I am dragging Calvin at the end of a Sonotube form. I am thinking a little bit about glory. A little bit about how far we have to go.

I hear Calvin say something.

I stop. Look back at him. I say, "What?"

He says, "I said, uh-oh."

Then I see. Matt Drinker and Lance Pierson. Taking long steps right at us. And Corey McSpirit is coming along behind them.

"Hey Butt-hole! Fetus-face!" Matt says. "Leave that! It's mine. I have a plan. I'm going to saw that up and hang the hoops for accuracy practice."

I get what he is saying. He wants targets. For lacrosse. It would be pretty fun to shoot balls through the circles.

I say, "If you're going to cut it up can't you use a few shorter ones?"

"Can. But I won't. That big one is mine."

Calvin says, "Well, wait a second. How good are you?"

Matt says, "What are you talking about?"

Over there to one side, quiet Corey McSpirit is smiling. He speaks up. He says, "That's a fair question."

Calvin says, "The greater test of accuracy comes with the smallest opening. Am I right?" I see Corey nodding his head. Calvin says it again. "So how good are you?"

Matt Drinker goes all red in the face. He says, "What do you know? You don't even play."

Calvin says, "Me? Heck no. I'd stink at that game. But I'm asking you. Sure you can send a ball through a twelve- or fourteen-incher. Easy. But what about that eight over there?" He points at the smaller tubes.

Matt says, "No way. I know what I want." He takes a step closer.

I say, "Come on, Matt." I point back toward the foundation. "There are plenty of tubes. I can get them for you. I can cut 'em—"

"Nope! That one is mine." He points.

Calvin says, "How do you figure? *Why* is this one yours?"

"Because, Pygmy Boy. It's closer to my house than to anyone else's."

Calvin shakes his head. He says, "That's *incomprehensible*." I see Calvin thinking. He tells Matt, "How about this? It's yours . . . *if* you can knock me off of it."

About a hundred holy cows go mooing inside my head. *NO-O-O-O!*

But don't you know it, Calvin dives onto that tube. Pins it to the ground. He wraps arms and legs around it. He locks his hands together. Hooks his ankles. Tucks his chin. Closes his eyes.

Calvin Chumsky is not going to let go of that tube.

chapter 28

THE FIGHT FOR
THE TUBE

I look at Calvin all attached to the Sonotube. Makes me think. Sometimes Uncle Drum watches sports. Basketball, soccer, or football. Of course, he has to get the TV from Shayleen now and that isn't easy. But what I am thinking about right now is who wins. Sometimes there is a better team. But sometimes there is a team that wants it more.

Matt Drinker lands on Calvin like a chest of drawers.

Lance Pierson hollers, "Crush him, Matty! Crush him!"

What a scramble! We got scuffing. We got pulling and clawing. We got Calvin grunting under the weight of Matt.

I am not one to let somebody pound on my best friend's scrawny back. I cannot stand to let him rip him out of his shirt. Or dig his nails into his bare skin like he is doing. So I go over and drag Matt off Calvin.

Matt turns and thumps a few punches on me. Tells me, "Quit touching me, you sweaty hog!"

Calvin says, "Let him at me, Mason. I can do it!" And he clamps his skinny self to that tube all the harder.

Matt grabs Calvin's shirt. Pulls that all out of shape. Both guys groaning. Struggling. Lance Pierson eggs Matt on. Corey McSpirit stands to the side. Keeps just one eye on the fight. Sick look on his face. I'm not good at figuring that dude out. But then Corey says it—kind of sharp. "Let him have the tube, Matt." One side of his lip curls up. Corey says, "We'll use the other ones." But Matt is deaf to him.

And then I feel like Corey is the same as me. I don't mean he is big with sweat pouring off him. Not that. I mean he doesn't like this scene. And we both know Matt won't quit. I turn to root for Calvin. And gosh, he holds on. But I see his fingers slip-slip-slipping. And I watch . . . and I watch . . . with my two fists full of sweat.

Blaaam! A car horn blasts. *Blaam!* I look and see the Drinkers' van rock to a full stop. Mrs. Drinker puts her head out the window. "Matty! Matty! Let go of that little boy! Let go right now!"

She gets out of the van. Matt lets go of Calvin. Mrs.

Drinker takes giant steps across the roughed-out drive-way of the building lot. She hollers for Matt, Lance, and Corey McSpirit to get into her car.

Matt hollers back. He says, "All right! All right! But you don't have to drive us. We can walk it. It's only two doors down!"

But Mrs. Drinker will not have that. She says, "You will get in the car!" Finally, he does. After Corey. After Lance. The door is the slow-slide kind. Lance has time. He leans up. Shows me his middle finger before the door seals them in.

Mrs. Drinker stays. She kneels down by Calvin. Taps on his arm. She says, "Are you all right?" She says it over and over again.

I hear him saying, "Yep. Yep." Little mouse sounds. Then bigger ones. He says, "I'm fine. Just resting. It was a friendly contest. Seriously. I'm fine."

When she believes him it's kind of funny because Calvin is still wrapped around that tube. Like he is glued on there.

I tell Mrs. Drinker, "If he says fine, he really is fine." Hope I'm right.

Mrs. Drinker goes back to the car. She takes Matt and his friends two doors down to the Drinker house. The garage door opens. Swallows them up.

I get down in the dust beside my friend. I say, "Calvin? Hey there. You really all right?" I tip my head down to see his face. Dirty. Muddy rings around his nose holes. He is a bit scraped up.

He stops holding the tube so tight. Soon, I think he is just lying on it. His eyes slide sideways to look right at mine. Smile opens across his face. Calvin says, "Mason, the tube is ours." And he starts to laugh.

We pick the tube up again. Swing and stumble. We have some good glory. We carry home that prize.

chapter 29

SAND AND PAINT

Saturday morning Calvin brings paint. Leftovers from their new house in the upper development. He comes down Jonagold Path dragging the two buckets on the road. Looks like his pencil arms will pull out of the sockets. I go to help.

I say, "Calvin, you are scraping a trail."

He grunts. "Would you take the buckets?" I do. But he still looks pretty weighed down. Still huffs and puffs. That is due to his heavy backpack. He tells me he has a bag of sand in there.

Pretty soon, we are in the root cellar. Flashlight shining. We are mixing that sand into the paint. It's a recipe Calvin learned off his tablet. The stirring feels good. Sand into the pale paint. We take turns to mix it. Then we start with two old brushes from our shed. We stroke the paint onto the root cellar walls. Thick and spready. It is the perfect thing. When I brush it on the wall I say, "Aww!"

Then Calvin says, "Aww!" Because this is perfect Caves of Lascaux paint.

We work awhile. Until Calvin drops his brush. He says, "Ugh." He makes a puking face. He says, "Mason, we have to *ventilate* or we're going to *die* in here."

I get it. Ventilate is about two things. The paint is smelly. And it needs air to dry.

I set down my bucket and brush. Rub my sweaty hands on my pants. I say, "We're going to have to open that door, huh?"

Calvin shakes his head. He says, "No way are we giving up our location. If they find out we are here, it'll ruin everything." He looks at me straight on. He says, "Let's never give up the root cellar, Mason. Not for anything. Tell no one." That is a dead-serious look on Calvin. Maybe because he feels like puke.

So I say, "I won't. I promise." Then I tell Calvin, "I have an idea."

The idea is this: We have the old tractor. And it runs. Sometimes. So I take Calvin up beside the shed where the tractor stays. Key is always in it. I hop up. Give it a start. That engine backfires first. A poof of stink sends Calvin running backward. Holding his nose. But now I know it'll run pretty great as long as it has fuel.

Turns out it doesn't have much. Or could be the gauge is off. But I set the throttle. Start driving it down to the dip. I am laughing because Calvin is jumping up and down. Running alongside to cheer me on. The tractor sputters and bucks. I tell it, "Come on, come on! Giddyap!" It goes. And goes. Rolls. And stalls out at the root cellar door.

I ask Calvin if that will be all right.

He says, "Perfect." But I don't know. The tractor is not that tall. But what Calvin thinks is this: The tractor is a *distraction*. Something to look at instead of looking at the door. And the door is open only about halfway anyway. And it is still under the cover of brambles. So okay.

There is air for Calvin. He stops feeling sick. Dip after dip, I load my brush the way Benny Kilmartin's dad Andy showed me. But this is a different kind of paint job. Dirt from the wall mixes in. Makes it look even more like the Caves of Lascaux on Calvin's tablet.

On we go. Load, stroke, and spread. Load, stroke, and spread. I work high. Calvin works low. Easier for me to put paint across the ceiling. I'm way taller. I watch out for the beams. Don't need another bump on the head.

I paint and paint. I think this: If I could do nothing else for the next one hundred hours, I would be happy. But for sure we will finish up faster than that. The root cellar is not so big.

Calvin says, "The recesses in the root cellar walls are

like the chambers. The real Caves of Lascaux had a good number of them. There was the Great Hall of the Bulls. And the Chamber of Felines, and the Shaft of the Dead Man." Calvin knows them all.

He has an idea about us burning sticks to make charcoal. He says we can draw animals on the walls.

I listen to him. A thought comes to my brain: We are making something awesome right *on* the property of the old Buttle farm. Adding something instead of subtracting. First time in a long time for that. Unless you count Uncle Drum adding Shayleen, and I would not. Shayleen, with her shopping channel Chia Pets and her flying-saucer salad bowl. All still in the boxes.

Calvin and I finish painting the last patch of wall. We sit down on our five-gallon-bucket chairs. Pick paint off our hands. We look around us. Clean pale walls.

I say, "It sure is different now."

"Transformed," says Calvin.

I say, "So hey. What about that Sonotube?"

Turns out Calvin has special paint for that. It is not just pale. It is white. All white.

He tells me, "The inside of the tube absolutely has to be a light color. *Reflective.* So it gives back the light. See how the brown of the cardboard is dark? Well, that is *absorptive.* It eats the light up."

I like the way he explains. I get it.

Calvin reaches inside one end of the tube with his

brush and I reach inside the other end with mine. I get my arm in deep. Up to the shoulder. Calvin too. Not so easy painting where you can't see. But it is funny.

Calvin tells me, "You just painted my hand, Mason. And you keep twisting the tube."

I say, "Yeah, well. How do you like my Caves of Lascaux knuckles?" I pull my arm out of the tube to show him.

He says, "Now your hands almost match your head."

I touch my head. Feels like plaster. But it is the sand paint from working on the ceiling. I say, "Looks like I dripped on your head today too."

Calvin says, "Yes. That feels like bird turds."

I say, "Looks like them too."

So we laugh while we paint that whole inside of the tube. Me trying to roll it one way. Calvin trying to roll it the other.

Then finally, he says, "There. I think we're done."

I pull my arm out of the tube. Feels like pulling my whole self out. Got a cramp in my shoulder. I use my shirt to wipe my face. I say, "Phew! What a job."

Calvin says, "Okay, so much for the easy part."

I make some wide eyes at Calvin. I wonder what's coming next.

chapter 30

BAD TIMING

Sunday morning, I cannot wait to get into the root cellar again. Got to see how the paint dried. But I won't go down there without Calvin.

I come out of the crumbledown with four pieces of toast in my hand. I wait by the edge of Swaggertown Road. Take a few bites. Watch for Calvin to come down Jonagold Path. Then I think this: Might as well go up and meet him. I take a look to my left. Then right. Check for cars. Don't you know it. There is one coming. Not too fast, I think. But I step back anyway. Then I see. It is a Merrimack Pee Dee cruiser. Another look and I see it: number 003. That's Lieutenant Baird. And now he is slowing down. Way down.

Sure thing. He pulls off Swaggertown. Tires crackle over the gravel right next to my feet. I hear the *swoosh*. The lieutenant's window going down. He hangs one arm out. Waves with two fingers.

I swallow hard. Toast crumbs in my throat.

The lieutenant says, "Good morning, Mason."

I say, "Good morning." In my head I think this: It *was* a good morning. Not so sure now.

He says, "Having a little breakfast, are you?"

I scuff my foot. I say, "Toast." Then I say, "And I'm waiting for someone."

He says, "Oh yeah? Who's that?" He turns his head. Looks up Jonagold Path. Just quick.

I say, "A friend. Calvin. Chumsky."

He says, "What are you planning?"

I think about that. We are planning plenty. But I will not give up the root cellar.

I say, "We just hang out." That is true enough.

I think this: The lieutenant does not usually visit on a Sunday morning. And maybe this is not a real visit. Maybe it is more like bad timing. Like, he was just coming along Swaggertown and saw me. But now he is here. I worry he will say he wants to go inside the crumbledown. Take a look at that notebook he gave me. I know I have not been good about putting anything into that for him. The feeling of pressure comes. I see the ugly green. Starts up in spots this time. They turn splotchy. I blink.

The lieutenant says, "Well, enjoy your breakfast. And your Sunday. Stay out of trouble. I'll see you soon."

I nod. His window goes up with a snap. Tell you what. I cannot believe that is all. I breathe. The green stuff goes away. The cruiser rolls onto Swaggertown Road. Gone.

Funny thing. I'm looking at Calvin Chumsky. He is standing at the bottom of Jonagold Path. I think he has been waiting to cross. He's got a granola bar in one hand and a garden trowel in the other.

I shrug. Show him that I have toast. Two pieces still. Both a little broken from me holding them too hard. And soggy from my sweaty hands.

Calvin crosses. We do not talk about the 003 cruiser. We have something else to do.

chapter 31

THE BIG DIG

Things are Sunday-morning quiet down in the Drinker yard. Just Moonie. Small black-and-white curl on a patio chair. Timing is good. Calvin and I slip behind the tractor. In through the bramble door. We sit inside the cellar and finish our breakfasts. Peaceful.

We look at our good work. The paint is dry. Mostly. Smell is gone. Mostly. Got Uncle Drum's flashlight propped in a recess on the back wall. Seems like more light in here than before. This is because of the pale walls. *Reflective* is what this is. Calvin promises there is even more light coming. He clicks on his tablet. Finds that light-shaft picture again.

What we have to do is this: First we have to go up on

top. Like we are standing on the outside roof of this root cellar. Second, dig a perfect circle hole all the way down to the wooden ceiling here on the inside of the root cellar. He points up.

Calvin says, "I think we'll hit the ceiling boards about five feet down. Maybe six. We have to keep the hole super perfect, Mason. We want the Sonotube to fit tight."

I tell Calvin, "We have to go down six feet? And wide as the tube? And you brought that little-bitty trowel?"

He says, "Yeah. I know. That's all we had at my house."

I tell him, "You can put that away. I got something else."

I fold my last piece of my toast into my mouth. Wipe my hands on my pants. Then I go search the shed. Lucky thing. I find the post-hole digger in that mess of tools all leaned up against the wall. I grab it. Then I go stand where Calvin tells me. In the brambles. All the way up to my shins. I take one look to check the Drinker yard. I am up high here. Anyone coming out that back door could sure see me. But it's just Moonie down there. I watch him stretch then curl up again. Then I look down between my feet. I plunge the digger in. Break ground.

Tell you what. It goes slow. But I dig clean. Keep the sides straight. Keep that hole wide enough for the tube. I lift the plugs of dirt out of the hole. One at a time. That's how it goes with the post-hole digger.

Calvin helps. Drags the pricker canes out of my way.

I dig down about two feet. Then I rest my sweaty cheek on my sweaty hands on the handles of the digger. Calvin thunks the tube into the hole. Never mind that the tube is taller than he is. He puts his arms around it. Big lift. Mighty Calvin. He twists it around in the hole. Hauls it out again. The tube makes a circle-mark down in the dirt. I know to follow that. Calvin talks about *precision*. I talk about this being the deepest hole I have ever dug.

We spend a long morning. Then take a lunch break. I'm a soaking wet gross-out. I change my T-shirt. I eat two sandwiches. Drink two glasses of milk. Calvin has one of each. We battle Shayleen for the last six vanilla wafers. We win all of those. Thanks to Grandma.

Back outside, the hole is deep. The digging gets crazy hard. Last eighteen inches takes the longest. I drop the digger into that hole. Bend my knees—full squat—and lift it out again. I pluck about a cup of dirt at a time. Slow go. Calvin's part gets harder too. The tube gets stuck lots. On the way in. On the way out. So I help. Finally, finally, I thump the digger into the hole—way down deep—and there is a sound. Like wood.

Calvin shouts into the air. He says, "That's it! You are there, Mason!" Then he is quieter to say, "You hit the ceiling of the root cellar! Sweet!"

We sink that tube one last time. Push down hard on it. It sticks up out of the ground just about one foot. Calvin says it's all good. We can leave it in place now. Then he sits his butt down on it. Looks like a baby on a potty. He wiggles his feet. The tan-sandy shoes. Gets me laughing.

But then he hops up again. Back to business.

We go down inside the cellar. We look up. He says, "One circle cut to go, Mason."

I tell Calvin, I get it. I know what to do. I know because of Benny Kilmartin's dad. Andy. Helped him cut the hole for their dryer vent. We had to match up the hole in the Sheetrock to the hole in the house siding. Indoors to outdoors. This light shaft is way bigger and deeper. But same kind of job. You drill, is what you do.

Lucky thing. The drill is charged up. Cordless. I stand on a bucket and reach up. I try to find the center. That's a little bit of hit or miss. Prayers and wishes, is what Andy Kilmartin said. I remember. Benny closed his eyes for a few seconds like he was doing both. Praying and wishing.

But Calvin keeps eyes open. To measure. He tells me where to try. I pray and wish. I drill. Then I stick a piece of coat hanger wire up the hole. Calvin runs up top. Looks down the tube to see where it comes out.

He calls down to me. And I hear him! Amazing! It's Calvin's voice coming down through the earth. And then I know. It is like we built a laundry chute. All I have to do is get this piece of wood out of the way.

Calvin says, "So close! Drill another hole just one inch to your right. Okay, Mason? To your right."

I hoist the drill up. Squint my eyes. Make the new

hole. I stick the wire in. Calvin shouts, "Yes! That's the middle! Perfect!"

Inside the cellar I boost him up. He draws a circle on the wood. Measures with his eyes and an old school ruler from our toolbox.

I say, "Hey. Looks a little small. Isn't our tube bigger?"

He says, "*Precisely.* This is smaller, so the wood will support the Sonotube. Like a lip for it to sit on. Otherwise, the tube could come falling straight into the root cellar. We've worked too hard for that."

I say, "Right."

Wish like crazy I had a hole saw. Even a small one to start punching this thing open. We had one. Once. Probably still have that somewhere. But the toolbox is not so in order. Can't even ask Uncle Drum. He's not home. Sunday is his longest day at the diner. He stays on for Stewart's turkey and gravy dinner.

So I go mad-wild drilling with the same little drill bit.

Calvin says, "Go, Mason! *Swiss cheese* that thing!"

I go around the circle Calvin drew. I put holes like where clock numbers go. Then more holes in between. Hard thing is drilling upward. Takes a lot of grunts. Dirt falls through the little holes. Hits me in the face. But I get all the way around. And then I drill a bunch of holes tight together. Make a slot.

I tell Calvin, "That should be big enough to fit the blade of the handsaw. All I have to do is saw along.

Connecting those dots until it's all cut open." Soon as I say it, I remember. I don't have that handsaw! I let out a squawk.

Calvin remembers too. We both say, "No handsaw!"

Calvin paws through the toolbox. Holds up a chisel. And a hammer.

Well. Tell you what. It is another big job. I drill more holes. Then I go all along the circle with the hammer and chisel. I blink my eyes to keep dirt and splinters out. Finally, finally, that circle of wood drops out. Hits me right in the lip. Down comes a shower of dirt.

Well. That lip smarts. Makes my eyes tear. I blink like crazy. Then I look. I see Calvin. He is standing right below the hole. And tell you what. There *is* light!

Holy cow.

chapter 32

END OF A DAY

You can guess it. Calvin and I are dirty after all our work. We have bramble scratches all up our legs and arms. But we stay. We take turns looking up through the shaft to the sky. It is all good.

Then Calvin says, "The dead man!"

I say, "What?"

He says, "The Shaft of the Dead Man! From the Caves of Lascaux. I can't believe I didn't think of it before! Remember that drawing of the stick man with a bird head on him? He was half lying down. With another bird nearby?"

I say, "Oh. Yeah."

Calvin says, "We should paint our own version of him

here. Maybe right on the floor where the light hits. It will shine right on him. *Yes!* The Shaft of the Dead Man! It's meant to be!"

Well, he might be right. But we cannot do that today. Sun is low. Calvin has to go home. Before dark. That's the rule. We take a five-gallon bucket. Turn it upside down over the opening at the top of the new shaft. Gotta have a cover. Keep out the rain. It sticks up some. But it doesn't look like much. We kick the loose brambles back over.

I say, "Guess we turned out the light. Down in the root cellar."

Calvin says, "Yeah. For now. We need one more thing to finish the light shaft off just right. I don't know what yet. We need a clear cover for the tube."

I say, "Like a five-gallon bucket with a glass bottom in it?" It is a joke. But Calvin doesn't laugh. He is thinking. Hard.

He says, "Hmm. *Something.* A bubble or a dome to cap it. Yeah, it really should be a dome. Because in *theory*, a curve will collect more light to send down the shaft."

I am thinking that sounds amazing. I am also thinking good luck to us finding one. We have looked inside the construction dumpsters plenty. Nothing like that in there. I start to think. What is in the shed? Then I think my way along the rows inside of Bishell's Hardware. And in Grandma's kitchen. Nothing.

Calvin and I soap up our scrapes and scratches at the

spigot. Stings like crazy! It is a whole day of good dirt running off us. Making a puddle. Then don't you know it. Up comes Moonie. All by surprise! He wags and crouches. Pushes between Calvin and me. About knocks us on our butts. We get tail slapped. He dances in the puddle. His pink tongue laps at the trickle from spigot. Calvin laughs. He says, "Drink! Drink! Drink! Moonie Drinker!" And Moonie does.

I say, "Moonie boy! What are you doing here? How did you get out? Is your gate open? Huh, buddy? Huh?" And that dog licks me like I am a steak bone. We give him chest scratches. Four hands on. It is nice that Calvin likes this dog. Pretty well.

Then I walk with Calvin—and Moonie—out to the road. I hook my finger under Moonie's collar. Just gentle. Just safe. I watch Calvin start up on Jonagold Path. I like to *see* that he is on his way. Going home for supper. Helps me feel all right.

I think this: Monday is coming. Another day at the cluster stop. Won't be bad. Calvin and I have a place. The root cellar. Keeps getting better in there. And Calvin has more plans. I like it. I still miss the limbs and branches in the tree fort. Maybe not as much now.

I take Moonie home. I wander the long way. Go through the Buttle orchard. I come to the tree fort. Still hard to look at that spot. The missing ladder. And to remember Benny at the bottom. And to wonder all over again how that happened. He was supposed to go home for supper, is all.

Funny thing the way Moonie stops. Sniffs the ground below the fort. I remember how Matt and Lance snuck up on Benny and me. Plenty of times. Creamed us in apples. It's one of those things. Seems long ago. But not long ago. But it was before Uncle Drum sold that last parcel. Boy. Benny Kilmartin would be surprised to know that so many new people moved into Merrimack. I think this: I wish Benny could be here to know Calvin. Wish that a lot.

I call to Moonie. He hops right to me. I say, "Good dog." Then I reach up to a limb. Pick two nice fat McIntoshes from the tree. I bite into one. Roll the other up ahead of us for Moonie. He chases. Tail high. Dives on the apple and brings it back to me. I throw it again. We do that all the way down to the Drinkers' house. No lacrosse players today. If I see Matt now, he will behave. He will be that other side of himself. No worries this time of day. When I am putting Moonie inside the fence, Mrs. Drinker opens the back door.

She says, "Oh, Mason!" She is glad to see me. She says, "I see that our Moonie Monster was out again. Hmm. Thank you for bringing him home." Then she says, "While you are here, can I count on you for Columbus Day weekend? We'll need a dog-sitter. Matty and I are going to see his dad."

I say, "Sure!" She knows it anyway. I will always say yes

to taking care of that dog. The glass door closes. I raise one hand. A good-bye.

Moonie looks after me. Me after him. Mrs. Drinker sets a bowl down for him. I turn to go. Glad I got Moonie home in time for his supper.

Then I notice that I am mad-hungry too. Wild-hungry! I pick up the pace. I want my supper too.

chapter 33

EXTINCT

On Monday in the SWOOF, Calvin is on the big couch. Or in it. Folded. He leans over his own legs. Looks at the Caves of Lascaux on his tablet. He shows me the pictures. Animals. I see the Black Horse. The Felines. Then something else. Very big.

I say, "Whoa! Whoa! Holy cow! What is that?"

Calvin says, "Well, it is a holy cow. Sort of. It's called an *aurochs*. It's like an ox. Or the ancestor to our cattle. But the aurochs is *extinct* now. You know. Gone forever."

I get that. I tell Calvin, "Same thing happened to apples. Did you know? Some varieties are gone for good."

Calvin says, "Really?" He thinks. Then he says, "That's

a crying shame." I think it is nice how Calvin cares about apples.

I say, "But you know what? There's some they thought were gone. But turns out they are still around. Like in really old orchards. And there's people trying to find them again. Maybe bring them back again."

Calvin says, "Well, good. They should."

We look at the pictures of the aurochs. Starts me wondering if there could still be one last one. Somewhere. Anywhere. Calvin tells me how to spell it. Thought it might end with X. I hear one. But it does not.

I say, "That's my favorite. Of all the cave animals. Right there." I touch my sweaty finger on the tablet. Leave a smear on the aurochs. Calvin doesn't care.

I don't know why I get such a feeling about that animal but it is like he is me. Like if he had to come to school he would be the biggest thing in the hallway. Like me. And I feel I am like him too. I feel just as huge. I even feel all red and brown. Not sure if someone could understand what I mean by that. It is from the inside to the outside. It is the strong part of me. Like I am full of heat and power. If I could meet the aurochs and touch him I bet he would feel warm too.

Calvin is making a plan about the root cellar. Knows what he wants to put on the pale walls. And on the floor below our light shaft. I lean down. Talk quiet to Calvin.

I say, "Hey, can there be an aurochs? Can it be *me* who paints it?"

Calvin says, "Of course!" He makes the big eyes. Round nose holes. Then he nods. Head and shoulders. Like he is the big giant body of that aurochs. Even though he is tiny Calvin Chumsky.

I am thinking of something to write. No one is using the Dragon. So I move to the squatty desk and set up. Tissue ears and potato fists. I rest my head. Close my eyes.

I talk to the Dragon:

So. Umm. I went by there again. The tree fort. Just walking Moonie Drinker home. Seeing it does not get better. I pretty much know that now. But umm there is something that does feel a little bit better. About the rest of my life. It feels like there might be not as much bad luck. All around me. Feels like it is turning. Changing. Or pushed back. Like there might be some cave where that stays now. Things probably don't work like that. But my mind shows me it like a picture. The best is being busy doing work. Umm. I mean with a friend. I think it is why I like being—

Suddenly, Annalissetta Yang is beside me. She yanks the tissue out from under my left ear. Her hands are curled but they are quick. She lifts the headphone and says, "Hop off, Mason. It's my turn to use the Dragon. I'm on the schedule."

I bang my knees on the underside of the desk. I'm trying to get out of her way. I know that I am not on the schedule. I stand up. She moves right in. She rolls her Crocodile over my foot. She says, "Oh, sorry. Sorry, Mason." I think she means that.

Ms. Blinny sees me getting up from the Dragon. She says, "Oh, come talk to me now. Wait. Did you remember to close out your profile, Mason?"

Annalissetta says, "Just did it for him." She is all settled in.

Ms. Blinny double-checks that. She says, "Okay. But Mason, try to remember to close out for yourself. And Annalissetta, maybe next time you could give Mason a little more time to wrap up." Then she points to the lava lamp. She says, "Oh! Cool! Giant mushroom, you guys. Don't miss it."

I watch the red mushroom. Slow rise. It splits in two. Makes hot orange halves. Then I go around the bookcase. Sit down at Ms. Blinny's desk. We talk about how things are going. She asks about home. I say, "Home is good." I'm thinking about the root cellar. I tell her Calvin Chumsky and I have a project. But I do not tell what. I don't give up the root cellar. Not even to Ms. Blinny.

She looks at the top of my head. She says, "Hmm. Have you been painting something?" Big-teeth smile.

I say, "Yes." I smile back.

She says, "Awesome! You've got a good buddy in Calvin, don't you?"

I say, "Yep." I tell her Calvin doesn't mind the things about me. Not the sweat. And the not-reading stuff. He doesn't mind the way it is at the crumbledown. I say, "He is good at explaining. He looks up everything. Does it on that tablet of his."

She says, "Yes. I've noticed that! Calvin is quick on that tablet. And you know what else I'm hearing?" She makes the giant smile. Right at me. She says, "He's got a good friend in you too, Mason."

Then she asks if Lieutenant Baird has been by. I tell her yes but no. Then I explain about seeing him at the edge of the road on that perfectly good Sunday morning. My bad timing. Ms. Blinny tilts her head and says, "O . . . kay. Hmm." Drums her fingers on her chin. I wonder if she is thinking what I am thinking. If he hasn't come lately, he will come soon. Just like he said.

I sit up all of a sudden. I say, "Ms. Blinny. Could you help? I have got to print something off that Dragon."

She says, "Sure we can! Right after Annalissetta finishes up."

I think this: Good. I will have something for that notebook. Something for the lieutenant.

chapter 34

THE LIEUTENANT

Tell you what. If you think on something you can bring it right to you. Not always. But sometimes. And it might be something you don't even want. From the window of the bus Calvin and I can see cruiser number 003. White with blue stripes. Parked at the crumbledown. So can Matt and Lance and Corey. And everyone.

Then the whole bus gets quiet. Except for Lance. He says, "Oooo. The cops are at Butt-face's house again."

I slump in the seat next to Calvin. I whisper. I tell him, "There won't be chasing today. No apple throwing. Not with the lieutenant there."

Calvin whispers back. He says, "I'll try not to be too disappointed."

I say, "Bad thing though. You cannot stay while I talk to him. So, can you make it on your own?"

He says, "It's like you said. They won't chase me. Not today. I'll wait on the porch in the mouse chair. When the coast is clear, I'll sneak down behind. I'll make sure no one sees me. You can meet me later."

I nod. I say, "I know where."

Then I sit in the kitchen with the black-and-white notebook in front of me. Orange pencil sticking out of a fold. And in that same fold I put my papers from the Dragon. Grandma looks at those. Just quick. Curious. Then she starts to clean. This is her thing to do while the lieutenant is here. She slides all her canisters forward. The toaster too. National Public Radio is off. She drags a damp rag along the back of the kitchen countertop.

The door has been shut on Shayleen. But I have seen before that she cracks it. Puts her eye or ear to the slot. Eavesdropping is what that is. Uncle Drum leans on the wall near the door. Mug of afternoon coffee in his hand. Lieutenant Baird has one too. Paper cup. Both of them eye those Dragon papers.

The lieutenant says, "So, what is this here, Mason? You're typing some of it now?"

I say, "Yeah."

He says, "Well, I'm glad to see this." He picks up the papers. He reads pretty fast. But it seems long. I wait. I swallow. I dry my face on the shoulder of my shirt. He says, "Okay. Okay. It's a little rough. Not *quite* what I'm looking for."

I think I know what he means. It is not enough about Benny. It is my story. I have not gotten to all of it yet. I don't think he'd be interested in the Dragon. So I don't tell about how that is where the typing is done.

He says, "But this is more than you've given me before. In writing. This shows that you can do it." He is a little loud about saying that.

Funny thing I am thinking here. All my talking comes out for the Dragon. The lieutenant is opposite. He interrupts, is what he does. Then my talking comes to a halt.

He says, "Well, this is good. Very good." He pulls out his phone and takes pictures of my pages. He looks at me. "You liked Benny and his dads, huh?"

I say, "I liked them a ton. I still do."

He says, "You did some chores there. Built some things together?"

I say, "Lots of times. I painted trim. Helped build the rock wall. I always liked helping with—"

The lieutenant interrupts. Again. He says, "Mason. Do you know that you can still help Andy and Franklin?"

Makes my chest warm when I hear it. I say, "I can?"

The lieutenant is nodding.

I say, "You mean work there? Like on the rock wall again?"

The nod turns to a headshake. No. He says, "What

they need is a different kind of help. They really need to know what happened to their boy, Mason."

And there goes the warm thing in my chest. Gone. And I feel stupid for not knowing this. The lieutenant wants help with his puzzle. The puzzle of how Benny died. I catch Grandma making thin minnow eyes at the lieutenant. I don't think she likes the way he said that to me. She balls the dishrag under one set of finger bones. Uncle Drum stares into his mug.

The lieutenant says, "Now, I know you say you found Benny at the bottom of the ladder. But what about just before that? You have something more to tell me about that. I know you do."

I take a paper towel. Blot my face. The towel sticks. I let it. Underneath that towel I start to see ugly green. I think this: There is *not* more. I was eating my supper. The Kilmartins called to see if I knew where Benny was. I said I would check the tree fort. I ran back through the orchard and found him. I have said it all before. I can't do it again. I don't want to see Benny the way I saw him. His neck. Don't want to remember how it was to try to make him breathe. I know I did it wrong. No air going in. You shut your lips over. Breathe. It is supposed to work. But I know it was too late. I held Benny in my arms. Could feel it. His life was gone.

I drag the paper towel down my face. Just slow. I see

pools of murky green. I wad the wet paper towel in my hands.

I think about what I told Ms. Blinny. Long time ago. I said, "I want to help the lieutenant. It seems like there is something I am supposed to say that will put his puzzle together. Like magic words that write themselves in glitter spills. Something. Something to make him stop coming to me."

She was drawing a swirl in the sand garden on her desk when I said that. She stopped still. Looked at me. Serious face on Ms. Blinny. She said, "Hey, Mason, I'm going to tell you something really important, okay?" Her eyes on my eyes. "Don't ever *invent* something for the lieutenant just because you think it'll make the questions stop. Only tell the truth. Okay? Promise me."

And I did promise her.

Now Lieutenant Baird says, "Do you like to play jokes, Mason? Do you like to laugh?"

I breathe. I say, "Well, you did ask me that before. Same thing now. I'm not that good at making up jokes. But I do like to laugh. Yeah." Then I think this: Does anybody *not* like to laugh?

Now Uncle Drum speaks into the kitchen air. Just quiet. He says, "Mason is right. We've been here before with all of this. You have seen his pages. The writing. I don't think he has anything more to tell you, Lieutenant."

Lieutenant Baird rises. Chair legs scuff the floor. He taps a finger on the notebook. He says, "Keep writing, Mason. I like that. Go ahead and type it out. Keep it all about your friend Benny. Good job."

Uncle Drum steps to one side to let him out the door. Grandma sets the dishrag in the sink. I wipe the paper towel ball along my neck. I look at Uncle Drum. The green stuff thins down to just kind of washy.

He says, "You did fine. You always do."

chapter 35

ONE STUCK WINDOW

Shayleen bursts out of my old room. She says, "Whoa! Thank god that cop is finally gone!"

For once I agree with Shayleen.

"I *so* need to pee!" She groans. "And I *so* need some fresh air! Man, close that door for too long and it gets stuffy." She fans her face. "Hey, Mason, that window is stuck shut again."

I say, "Yeah. Most of our windows are."

She makes bug eyes at me. She says, "Well? Can you open it? Puh-leeze?"

"Don't use that tone on Mason. He doesn't deserve it," Grandma says. But Shayleen is gone—into the bathroom. I am off to jimmy that window. The sooner she's happy, the sooner I get outside. I want to catch up with Calvin.

I stop to look around my old room. Shayleen has transformed it. In a bad way. Stuff everywhere. No place to set your feet down. The TV shopping channel is blabbering about some fill-a-gree necklaces. Eighteen-carrot gold, whatever that means. I mumble back. "How about some eighteen-turnip gold? Some eighteen-rutabaga gold."

Then I kick aside some brown packing papers. Step over a cardboard box. And another. My foot lands on a sheet of bubble wrap. *Pop! Pop-pop!* Bubbles. What is it about bubbles? And clear stuff? Wasn't there something important going on that had to do with bubbles?

This is what happens. Lieutenant Baird comes and my brain runs blank. I lose time. I scoot two boxes along the floor so I can get to that window. I look out and see the lieutenant's cruiser. Number 003. Rolling out onto Swaggertown Road. I think this: Good. He won't be back until the end of apple season. Bet you that.

I try the window. Shayleen is right. It sure is stuck. I turn my face to one side and grip the sash. I jiggle it. Rock it. Grunt at it. While I am doing that I see that unopened box. The one with Shayleen's plastic-saucer salad chiller in it. What a stupid thing that is. The picture shows it. Nothing but a huge plastic bowl. Who needs it?

Ha!

The window shoots up with a bang. Then it sticks there. I reach right down for the box with the salad thing in it. Scoop that up. Push it right out the window.

Done.

Just before Shayleen sees.

I walk toward her as she comes back in the room. I point my thumb behind me and I tell her, "Got it. Got that window open." Then I point at the TV screen. Flick my finger at it. I say, "Look at that. Some eighteen-carrot fill-a-gree neck chains. Look, Shayleen."

She looks. I slide by. I'm out of there.

chapter 36

CAPPING THE SHAFT

Calvin reaches both arms around the salad chiller bowl. Out of the box. He tells me, "Mason! This is perfect! It's the cap for the shaft!"

I say, "I knew it! Wasn't even looking for it. But then there it was."

Calvin says, "The Universe is amazing. It knows what we want. And sometimes . . . just sometimes . . . it hands it right over like a gift."

I think this: I'm not sure about the Universe. Because. Well. Some things are gone. *Bing. Bang. Boom.* So then what is there to say about the stuff the universe takes away? I try to think. What is the opposite of a gift?

Well. We have this salad chiller bowl, and I guess

Calvin is right. It is a pretty great gift. Calvin looks it over. So wide. It seems near as big as him. But everything is near as big as Calvin. Except for all the things that are just plain bigger.

Thinking of the bowl as a gift makes my heart rest easy. I do feel bad for stealing off Shayleen. Seems wrong on the one hand. But tell you what. She won't know it's gone. I dry my face on my shirt. Then my hands on my pants.

Calvin asks me, "How did it go? With the lieutenant?" He asks this like he wishes he didn't have to ask it.

I say, "Same as every time." I ask Calvin, "You know why he comes?"

Calvin shows a little mouth twitch. He says, "Well, you kind of told me before. It's about Benny."

I say, "Yeah. The lieutenant has questions. For the investigation. He thinks I can help him because I was there. Like, before. And then after." I wait. Then I say, "And Benny was my best friend. Guess you know that from the poems. And me talking about him. The lieutenant wants me to write it down. Hard for me. I feel like I told him everything. As best I can. I might do better if he didn't interrupt."

Calvin says, "Being interrupted is the worst."

I say, "Yeah it is! I don't know what more to say about it anyway. So at least now I can tell it to the Dragon and the Dragon doesn't interrupt." Calvin nods. But we don't say more about Benny. No more about the lieutenant.

We spy out the root cellar door. Coast is clear. We go up top and try that salad chiller bowl out. We set it upside down over the top of the tube. Doesn't sit so straight. Slips to a tilt. No matter what. Calvin thinks we need adhesive. I find some in the shed. Two tubes. Both wrinkled up. Split open and bone dry. I tell Calvin, "Bishell's Hardware will have it. I can pay for it. I have some dog-sitting money from Mrs. Drinker. And more coming after Columbus Day."

So we leave that bowl sitting as best it sits. In the root cellar the light shines down the shaft. Might be a little bit better than before. Because of the curve of that bowl. Not sure. But Calvin Chumsky smiles up at it. Nice clear cap for his light shaft.

chapter 37

THE BIG PINK CLOUD

I am set at the Dragon. I am full of something to say. I put my head down and start.

Okay. Today I am thinking about light. Shafts of light.
Because I got reminded about something. Something
Benny Kilmartin said. A story he told. About that kind of
weather when the clouds are dark. But then the sun puts
stripes of itself down. Down from some holes in the clouds.
Umm. It's like. Beams. Sunbeams. Coming through.
Yeah. So Benny said those are pathways. For people who
die. The sunbeams are a way to get to heaven. So then I
wonder if dead people have to lie below the shaft of light to
get up there. Or do they climb. Like a ladder. So like maybe

that is why a dead man would lie in a shaft. Like in the
Caves of Lascaux. Dead man with a bird head. He could
be waiting for the light to take him to heaven. And maybe
Calvin will know that for sure. From his tablet.

I stop a minute. I think this: My story is mixed. Some
things are past things. Some are right now. It happens
because one thing makes me think of the other. I guess
that's okay. Better than being stuck.

I talk again:

So there was the lieutenant again. Just the other day. At
the crumbledown. Asking the questions. It is getting harder
now. Months going by. Like my brain is not hanging on so
tight to the way it all was. Sequence. So umm I wonder
what if I went back to that part again. And what I mean
is the last part. When I ran in for supper. Trouble is that
is the part gets the lieutenant upset. From that first time I
tried to tell him. Way back. There was the thing that made
Benny laugh. So hard. And what it was is how I skipped the
ladder. I jumped down from the tree fort. Like too much of
a jump. The kind of jump makes your arms go in a circle.
Because you took too much air. And you need to do some
flying right about then. Only. You are no bird. So then
something in you knows you better roll. When you land.
Roll your body. Roll out of trouble. That is how it was. I did
that. Went rolling something wicked. My heels went right

over my head. Two times. But I got right up on my feet. Standing again. Had apple blossom petals stuck all over me. Head to toe. And then I turned around. Saw Benny. Leaning out. Watching me. And he hollered to me. Mason. Are you all right? And I hollered, Yeah, I'm okay. And then Benny well he laughed. Enormous. And that laugh came out of his mouth in a huge pink cloud. Color of raspberries. Big puff in the orchard. And that is not the first time I saw some pink all around Benny Kilmartin. But it was the hugest. Hugest. Because pink is the color of laughing. Of joy. Of a friend.

I stop talking. Grind my forehead into my potato fists. This is going pretty okay. I should keep at it. I tell the Dragon more:

Umm. So. Trouble is. That is the part the lieutenant did not like. The pink. He does not think that is a true thing. Made him mad. At me. So I don't tell that part to him anymore. Umm. Yeah. I skip about the pink cloud that came out of Benny's mouth. And too bad. Because that was the most amazing of all the pink I have seen.

So umm. A few times now the lieutenant asked me. All big and loud. Why did you jump, Mason? And the answer is because I was not smart. The jump was too far. Tried to say that to him. Tried to say what I hollered to Benny before I left. Which was: Don't try it. But the lieutenant was talking over my words. He said, Wasn't it because you knew something was wrong with that ladder? Isn't that why you jumped? Then he wanted to know did I throw away a handsaw. That one I had. From my birthday. He wanted to know did I toss that somewhere. In the orchard. In a ditch. And well I was thinking why would I do that? I said I did not toss it. But might be I did lose it. Somehow. And then he said I bet you did. And that was another time when Uncle Drum said we talked enough. And then the lieutenant asked me if I wanted to know why Benny fell? And I said yes. I figured he knew the puzzle. But umm he said something else. He said there was a weak rung on that ladder. And it broke. And he says I probably knew that. But I didn't. I was pretty sure I built that ladder right. Apple ladder. Pretty tall one. Eight steps. Two nails in each side of those. I bought the wood and nails brand-new. At Bishell's Hardware. And I got on it when it was done. Before Benny. To check it. Because I am way bigger. So if it would hold me it would hold Benny. Easy. So. Umm. Maybe I would have known when something went wrong with that rung. But I was not much for using the ladder. Because I am pretty good at climbing trees and dropping myself down from the branches. The ladder was for Benny. So. Umm. Well. And then the lieutenant asked me that same thing again. How did you decide you needed to jump down? Instead of climbing down on that ladder. Mason.

How? I said I didn't need to jump. I just did. And then I said
the same thing as before. Again. I said it was not smart.
Jumping down like I did. That part of the tree is too high.
I said nobody should try that. I tell the lieutenant that part
every time. But he still keeps coming back to ask.

chapter 38

THE CHUMSKY HOUSE

The Chumsky housekeeper is Margie. She watches us. Close. She is not new in Merrimack. She is old here. She gives me the sad-to-see-you look. Like she knows my story. About my family living in the old crumbledown on Swaggertown Road. How we have been selling off chunks of the orchard to developers. How my best friend died. I know people feel bad about it.

I used to see Margie at the diner. All those years of Saturday mornings when I went with Uncle Drum. Saw her at Benny Kilmartin's funeral too. Along with pretty much everyone. Used to be that most people in Merrimack knew most other people in Merrimack.

Now I am seeing her here. First time I am at the Chumsky house. We are here to make charcoal. Calvin learned it from his tablet. The way to do it is you burn some apple sticks. We got plenty from the orchard. Calvin said, "See that? We want apple wood and the Universe provides it."

I said, "Right. And maybe it is provided by my family too. The Buttles who came before me. The ones who planted the orchard. Before the place even had a first apple season." Calvin said I made a good point about that.

Now we take sticks. Same size as fat pencils. Just use the pruners. Found those in the shed. And I know which branches to take. Straight-up suckers. Uncle Drum used to say it. Those are robbing the tree. So they get cut out. It is a lot of seasons now that we have not taken care of this. The suckers are fat and they have gone from green to woody.

We peel the bark. Put the sticks inside a can. It is one that Calvin's mom saved. The kind from chicken broth. It has got a few holes punched in it. We put the can in a fire. One we built inside the fireplace at Calvin's house. Theirs works. That's why we are here. We've got a fireplace at the crumbledown too. It's old. It's stone. But something is wrong there. Something in the chimney, I think it is.

Margie stays close while we burn the fire. I try to smile at her. A couple of times. She looks away both. It is sort of like the sad-to-see-you. Pretty soon I get two feelings:

Warm fire on my face. Cold eyes on my back. Not sure why.

The charcoal takes a pretty long time to be made. Hours. That's what Calvin read. It has to *carbonize*. That will take until that fire goes cold. So we let that burn for the whole afternoon.

Calvin gets out pencils. Paper. And a roll of paper towels for my sweat. We sit down with the tablet and copy the shapes of that aurochs. And the dead man. We try to make them look like the ones in the Caves of Lascaux.

Margie looks over. Now and then. She doesn't ask about the drawings. Just as well. We won't have to say anything about the root cellar. She folds the Chumsky laundry. Starts their supper. When I get up to go home to my own supper, I say good-bye to her.

I say, "Nice to see you again. After so long."

She nods. But it's small. Wonder if she knows that I just lied some. Seeing her did not feel that nice.

I look at the fire before I go. Red embers. I tell Calvin, "Can't wait until it is charcoal. Tomorrow."

chapter 39

THE BAD DAY IN THE DINER

I sit at the Dragon. Ms. Blinny is pretty right about how this works. If I think about something before I tell it here, well, it comes out smoother. The story feels ready. It writes itself. From my voice.

So umm. I have been thinking. Remembering. Here is what. People used to be glad to see me. Even though I was this big sweaty kid. I think people liked me. Better. Before. Like Irene at the diner. In her hairnet. She always greeted me. Smiling. Stewart at the griddle too. But then we had a rough day in there. Not too long after Benny died. Both his dads were in the same morning Uncle Drum took me. A Saturday. I think it was. Andy and Franklin were at the corner table. And it was the first time I saw them after the funeral. I took myself right over to them. I said hello. I asked how was everything at their house. I asked about the stone wall. I just wanted to know. Was everything still the same. Or umm more like was anything still the same. Because tell you what. It didn't seem like it was. Not for me. I was missing Benny so much. Thought I could tell them. But Andy he umm he just kept two hands around his coffee cup. Stared down into it. Never did look up. Franklin is the one who said it. Mason. Please understand. We just can't talk to you. It's too hard. Then he said could I leave them in peace. And I thought of the other kind of peace. Like pieces of pie. Because there is that case full of pies in the diner and my brain just umm took the wrong bus on that. But umm well what he meant was stop talking. Stop talking to them. He told me better if I go over to my own table. I remember because then Uncle Drum came up and gave a tug on me. We went and sat down. But Andy and Franklin got up. Left their corn cakes. Full stacks. They held tight to each other. Both their sets of shoulders were umm well kind of stuck in the one doorway. Two grown-up men. So sad. And shaking too. And Uncle Drum tapped on the table in front of me. He whispered for me to stop staring. But well it was hard to stop that because I needed to see them. And I know mostly you wouldn't want to do this but umm I wanted to let the sad part worm all the way through me. Like getting it over with. Even though it was probably going

to take longer than anything in the world. I thought Andy
and Franklin were probably the ones that missed Benny like
I did. I felt the same as them. So then. Oh. Yeah. And then
on their way out Andy's elbow. Or his hip. I don't know.
But that caught on the gumball machine in the entry. Holy
cow. What could have happened then. I almost jumped up.
But Franklin he stopped and turned back to put that thing
steady before it could fall. Then they went out. Anyways.
It was like that whole diner froze over. I looked around the
place. Everyone there looked back at me with the sad-to-
see-you faces. Sad to see you is not what people say. But
they look that way. Now. So. That night I heard Drum tell
Grandma something. He said, Having a broken heart is no
excuse to break someone else's. Our boy is hurting too. He
meant me. Their boy. But. Well. Funny thing. What he said.
Because tell you what else hurt. Uncle Drum quit taking
me to the diner. He didn't say why. But seems like that was
because if people were going to just be all sad to see me
then maybe better if I not go in there. Anymore. So that
is how I umm I lost one of my places. I only see the diner
from the bus now. Only see it on the loop through town.

chapter 40

DISTURBING

Calvin and I run into the crumbledown from the cluster stop. We have banana milkshakes at the kitchen counter.

Shayleen comes out to bother me about a box she thinks will come today. Something she ordered. UPS. She says, "Will you be around, Mason? Can I count on you to bring it in?"

I say, "Could be I won't." I say, "You got your button boots on, Shayleen. Go out to meet Jerald yourself. He won't bite."

I think this: That girl needs to leave the house some. Before she goes pale and sick. Now she is cross at me. I don't have time for her. Calvin and I slide off the kitchen stools. Head out.

We check for the coast to be clear. We look for trouble first. Then both ways for cars on Swaggertown Road. Then we cross and go up Jonagold Path. We go into Calvin's house. Margie is running the vacuum cleaner. She nods at us. But she doesn't shut it off to talk. Fine. This is a quick stop. Just to get the can of apple wood out of the ashes. Charcoal. All black now. Calvin fishes one stick out of a hole. Gives it a pinch. It smudges him up. He smiles. He says, "Yes! It worked! *Carbonized!*" And we know we can use it to draw the great aurochs and the dead man on the root cellar walls.

He carries the charcoal can like it is a treasure. One hand on top. One hand on bottom. We come back down from Jonagold Path. Don't you know it, there is Moonie. Curled in that mousey chair on the porch at the crumbledown. He stands. Front paws start marching. Tail wagging so hard he will about fall over. My heart goes soft. This dog. He has been waiting for me. He comes off the busted steps. Out to meet us at the edge of Swaggertown Road. Not a good place for a dog. So I take his collar. Just gentle. Call him as we go. He comes.

Now I have this worry. I want to be with Moonie. Don't want him to be lonely. And he must feel lonely on account of how he came up the hill on his own. But

Calvin will want to be in the root cellar. Trying out that charcoal. And part of me wants that too.

I don't have to say it. Calvin knows. He says, "Think we can sneak the pup down without giving the place up?"

I say, "You mean bring him in with us? Inside you-know-where?"

Calvin laughs. He says, "Sure."

But then we don't even make it around the corner of the crumbledown. Because trouble comes up fast.

Matt Drinker is on the hill. I feel Moonie pull to a stop. Matt hollers. He says, "Buttle! What do you think you're doing with *my* dog? Took him again! Didn't you?"

I say, "No. Just bringing him back. Away from the roadside."

Lance Pierson hops to the front. Swings his lacrosse stick. At Calvin. He hits the charcoal can right out of Calvin's hands. There that goes. Spinning up into the apple trees. It pings off a limb. Lands in the grass. And there is Calvin. Mouth open. Hands empty.

That's bad. But I know what is worse. Worse is, the five or six more lacrosse kids who come up the hill behind them. Not because they will join in. No. It is usually just the two. But Matt will make a show of this. And he does. He throws down his own stick. He comes after Moonie. I step up front. Dog goes back behind my legs. I am looking for Corey McSpirit. He's not around.

Matt shoves me back. Grabs Moonie's collar. In a twist. A choke, is what. He starts in on him. He says, "Bad dog! Bad, bad, dog!" And it is awful. Moonie gets low. Licks his lips. And then Matt lands a smack on that poor dog's head.

I step up again. I say, "Hey, Matt. Hey."

He jerks Moonie by the neck. Swings him side to side. Moonie's feet have to go fast. Stepping left. Stepping right. I hear the small cry from him. No bark. More like a mew from a kitten.

I tell Matt, "Hey now. It's not his fault. Just be nice to him. Come on, Matt. Please."

Matt says, "If you don't like it, then quit letting him out of my yard, Butt-head! Because this is what he's gonna get from me every time you do it." Then he hits Moonie across the nose. Dog goes low. Eyes blinking.

There is a group grunt from those lacrosse dudes. Then a lot of quiet. I'm thinking and thinking. The inside of me is boiling. And tumbling. I don't think anyone likes this. Seeing a kid be bad to his dog. But no one steps up to say it. I want to tell Matt he is dead wrong. But I don't want to make this worse for Moonie.

So I say, "Okay. Okay. I won't come for him, Matt. But just be easy on him. He's a good dog. He's a really good one."

Matt says, "No. He's *bad*."

Then Calvin puts his small hands in the air. Voice up loud. He says, "Matt, I get how you feel because you're a basically *ignoble* kind of kid."

Lance Pierson says, "Shut up, Fetus-face. Don't try being all nicey-nice. We're not having it."

Calvin smiles. Just small. He says, "Okay, then just listen. Matt, Mason did not take your dog. We weren't even here. And we certainly have *not* been down to your house."

Lance pokes a stick at Calvin. He says, "Of course you're gonna stick up for Butt-hole."

Calvin says, "I am *vouching* for him. Mason didn't let Moonie out. The problem here is that the dog is smart. He knows who he wants to—"

Calvin stops. Like he changed his mind. He reaches down. Quick. Picks up Matt's lacrosse stick. And don't you know, Matt lets go of Moonie! He jerks the stick away from Calvin.

I think, Yes! Calvin is the smartest kid ever! Moonie scoots under my legs. I scoop him up. Take a few steps back. Holding him in my arms. And there we all are. Frozen in place.

Funny thing when nobody knows what will come next. Big surprise when the thing that comes is Uncle Drum. He drives up in the truck. Opens the door and slides out. Moonie lifts his nose. Smell of breakfast in the afternoon air.

Uncle Drum looks us over on his way to the house. He puts eyes on Calvin. Sees me with Moonie. Matt. Lance. And then the lacrosse dudes. He says, "Hello. Hello, boys. Hello, Moonie." He goes into the crumbledown. Shuts the door behind him.

I feel Moonie breathing. Pant-pant-pant in my arms. I think about the Universe. Seems like Uncle Drum was our gift just now. It's not that he did anything. Just showed up.

Matt says, "Put my dog down, Mason. Right now."

Calvin says, "Let's walk him back. Let's *all* do that. That way, all of you will know he's back home. And Mason and I will know he's not near the road. Or some other bad thing."

Calvin does not wait for an answer. Me neither. I keep Moonie in my arms. I start walking. This dog is good about being carried. Paws flopping. Ears too. The others follow. Matt shoves us along some. I feel a lacrosse stick in my back. Lance Pierson takes his stick and tucks the basket under Calvin's butt. Lifts up. Like he's putting him in a spoon. The tan-sandy shoes hurry forward.

Moonie licks my face. Matt says, "Disgusting! Dumb dog! Licking up Buttle's sweat. Ew!"

There is a lot of gagging behind my back. Fake barfing. I think this: Yeah. Well. I don't care that I am a gross-out. Moonie is safe.

At the Drinker gate I push ahead some. I want to see Matt's mom and I want to know that Moonie is inside. I want to see Mrs. Drinker take him in herself. And she does that. She is some surprised to see us all there. The lacrosse players walk on by. Into the yard. Start passing a ball.

Mrs. Drinker calls Moonie a Houdini. She says, "You're going to have your hands full for Columbus Day weekend, Mason!"

I smooth my hand over Moonie's head. I say, "He'll be good for me."

Calvin and I head off quick. Close the gate. We leave Matt and the others on the inside. We start up the hill. Calvin whispers. He says, "Careful. They could be watching."

I say, "Yep." I know what he means. I won't give up the root cellar. I won't even look at the place where the tractor is. Boy. It is hard to keep from doing that once your brain gets going on it.

I say, "The charcoal. Let's go find that first. I think I know where it landed."

Calvin says, "Me too."

Then we both look behind us. Over our shoulders. Don't you know it, Lance Pierson sticks one arm over the fence. Shows us his middle finger. We walk on.

Up by the crumbledown we start a search. Comb the

grass back under the McIntosh trees. We look for the can. Calvin is quiet. I ask him why. He says he is thinking. About Matt Drinker.

I say, "And Lance too? After what he did? Knocking away the charcoal can?"

Calvin says, "No, not so much that. I can defend myself. I have a voice. But what Matt Drinker did to his dog, that's different. It is *disturbing*."

Tell you what. *Disturbing* is a word that goes way inside. Close to my bones.

chapter 41

DRAWING THE AUROCHS

I am standing in the root cellar. Looking at the pale wall.
I have a stick of charcoal. Carbonized. Keep running
my finger along that. I keep closing my eyes. Calvin clicks
around on his tablet. He says, "Do you want me to bring
up that image of the aurochs?"

I say, "No. I don't need the photo. I see him. The
aurochs. I'm not sure why. But he's right there when I shut
my eyes."

Calvin says, "Hmm. Well. Okay then. Don't let that
blank wall stop you, Mason. Have at it."

Maybe Calvin knows that I don't want to make a
mess of the clean pale paint. Can't help thinking how
the Buttles have been. The way we've been subtracting

instead of adding. The root cellar is different. It is a place with progress to it. True since the day Calvin and I opened the door.

So I do it. I put the first charcoal mark down. And it is a long line. The long back of the aurochs. I walk a full step to make it. I put a dip in the middle. I like how the charcoal stick feels. How it is soft and gives itself onto that wall. And I go. I put up the lines my brain remembers. One after the other. I close my eyes. Then open them. Big parts first. That's how this is going. It looks right. Then it does *not* look right. But I think that is because I have to finish what I started. So I add the low belly. Then I add wideness to that rump—and don't you know it, a bump in the wall helps with that. Like it is meant to be. I draw the hinds of the aurochs. Can't believe it. Looks like I have done them right.

I draw a line upward. That's his chest. Then I draw the throat of the aurochs. His snout. Then the sloping face. I listen to the charcoal whispering along the wall. I draw pretty much a cap of a head. Like something I could cup my hand over—if I got myself close to an aurochs. But I won't. He is *extinct*. I step back and breathe. Next would be the eye. But I am not so ready to draw it. I give him his legs. The thick upper and thin lower. The knobby bend in the hind ones.

It is now that I hear myself. I have been humming. Grunting. Snorting like an ancient cow—the aurochs.

When I turn I see Calvin is not drawing. He is watching. And listening.

He whispers, "Don't stop, Mason!" He makes a rumble in his throat. Like me. Like the aurochs. He points to the wall and says, "The horns!"

So I turn back. Got that charcoal in one hand. The piece is smaller now. I raise both arms, curl my hands like the horns of the aurochs. I dip my head. Keep a rumble in my throat. I reach up and draw one curved horn. Then the other. And those horns look right! I have the feeling of this whole thing coming together. I pull my arm back. I take the stump of charcoal and drill through the air right to the face of the aurochs. I set down the mark that makes the eye. Then I roar. The sound goes off the close walls in the root cellar and back at me.

Holy cow! I feel mighty!

Calvin's eyes are wide and his mouth is open. Grinning. He stamps his tan-sandy shoes on the dirt floor. He says, "Yes! Mason! You *are* the aurochs!"

I make the sound of thunder. Stampeding hooves. I am loud. Calvin is cheering . . . and then there is another noise. It's sharp. And short. And we stop to listen. It is a bark!

Once. And again. And there is a scuff-scuffing noise too. Calvin looks at me. I look back at him. We are still and silent in the secret of the root cellar. The bark sounds again. We know who it is. We know what he's asking. It is killing me. I want to throw the door wide open.

Calvin puts his eye to the knothole. Walks his body one way. Then the other. He gives me a nod, like I can open the door. But he also presses his hands toward the ground, like to say, *Be careful.*

What you do then is you hope. Hope that the dog is here on his own. And you hope you didn't give up the root cellar while you were being the aurochs.

I am slow and careful about the door. I pull it open. Just inches. Two white paws scratch at the crack. A black nose squeezes in. Then Moonie leaps! He bursts in. I grab the rope. Pull the door closed behind him.

Well, now we have him inside, and tell you what, he is happy. He comes to me. Stands two feet on my knee. He stretches up. Tries to lick my chin. Then he bounces away and up to Calvin for more pats.

He runs around sniffing the corners and crannies of the root cellar. It's like he has too much to do. And it all must be done.

Tell you what. I can't help how much I love having Moonie with us. Calvin seems pretty okay with it too. Maybe he worries. Like me. Like what happens if Matt and Lance come looking for him. But we don't say it out loud. I just pull the door again. Shut it extra hard.

Moonie stands below my aurochs. He walks up close. Sniffs the fresh charcoal. His tail wags. Then he takes two steps, picks up his hind leg, and pees on the wall. Calvin and I laugh. We sputter and snort. We pinch our noses some because . . . *pee-eww*. But the piddle runs down the wall and soaks into the old dirt floor. The stink goes with it pretty quick.

Then Moonie goes and gives the old rag rug a scratch with one paw. It's just a thing I found kind of half under our porch where we forgot about it. He circles then lies right down. Chin on paws.

Calvin says, "I think he just moved in."

I say, "Guess so." I lean down. Pat that dog. That smell of him—not the pee, but that fur and skin smell—makes the middle of me warm. It is simple. I feel good with Moonie in the root cellar. It's like he belongs here. I know Matt Drinker would say different. I make a plan to carry Moonie home again. Give him protection. Right to his door. I will put him inside the Drinker house myself. But not yet. Because he has tucked his nose into a fold of the old rug and closed his eyes.

Moonie sleeps beside the aurochs.

chapter 42

THE DEAD MAN

Calvin is showing me some colors. He brought crayons, but not little-kid crayons. No. These are oil crayons. For artists. The colors are rust and brown and gold like our orchard in fall. The oil in them smells good, like the tractor and the lawnmower. Calvin says, "Try them out. You can smudge them and smear them. If you want to."

So I squat down by the wall. Begin to put some color on the aurochs. Calvin stands under the shaft. Tablet nearby. He gets down on hands and knees to draw the dead man. We work. Moonie sleeps with legs twitching. I think about those four boys. The ones Garrison Keillor said discovered the Caves of Lascaux. And that dog that was with them. The dog called Robot. I make it up in my mind—a dream for Moonie Drinker. He is running down a rocky hole in France. France over in Europe. He enters the cave and barks for his boys to come see what he sees. An aurochs on the cave wall. Like this one that I am dotting up with oil crayons, only a real ancient one. Moonie Drinker could do that. He could be the dog who discovers an art cave. He has that much dog greatness in him. I believe that.

It's not too long before I ask Calvin. I say, "Why do you think it was easy?"

He says, "Easy? What do you mean?"

I say, "For a kid like me to draw a pretty good aurochs. I mean all of a sudden like that. You know me. I'm good at making a tractor go. I can dig you a hole. That's me. I am no artist. But I made a pretty good aurochs here. Didn't I?"

Calvin says, "It's a *great* aurochs." He says, "You were in deep there. You were *feeling* like the aurochs, heart and soul. Your spirits must be matched, Mason. He's your symbol."

I jump up to say it. I tell Calvin, "Yes! That is what I think! This whole time, I thought it!"

I'm too loud. Moonie wakes and looks at me. He stretches. He curls himself opposite way now. Settles back down.

I tell Calvin, "So then what about you?"

Calvin says, "What about me?"

I say, "Why do you think about that dead man so much."

Calvin stands up. Looks down at his drawing. He says, "Well, that's due to a few things. First, it was a cool coincidence that we ended up with a shaft here in the root cellar when the Caves of Lascaux have the area called the Shaft. And the fact that the dead man is in there, and that he's the only human image at Lascaux. It's *intriguing*. From what I read, no one is sure why he's there. But you have to believe that the artists had a reason. He must be important. Even though he is skinny as a stick. Like me. But no worries, Mason. He's not my symbol. Not like you and the aurochs. I'm not the dead man."

That is a good thing to hear. I step over to Calvin. Look at the photograph on his tablet. The dead man. Then I look at the root cellar floor. Just below our light shaft. Calvin has drawn a pretty great dead man there in charcoal. The outline. With his weird head that is like a bird's head. The face that looks like it has a beak. I look at the photo again. I look at the body of that dead man. I say, "That dead man from Lascaux. Well. He sure has a pointed *thing* on him. You know that, Calvin?"

Calvin nods his big nod. He looks at the tablet.

I say, "Art is like that. Sometimes it is naked. Right?"

Calvin says, "Sometimes."

I say, "Are you going to draw that? On him?"

Calvin says, "Well . . . it seems important. So . . . I guess I will."

I say, "I think it's fine if you do. We are not at school. It probably wouldn't be allowed there. But here, nobody's going to see it. You and me. That's it." Then I say, "What about the bird? Not the one that is part of his face. The one on the stick beside him." I point. I touch the tablet by accident again. Leave a smear of oil crayon. Brown. Calvin never cares.

He says, "The bird is important too. Do you know what they say about that?"

I think and then I say, "No. I don't think Garrison Keillor told anything about the bird. That talking bit he did about Lascaux was pretty short."

Calvin says, "Well, for thousands of years, humans have believed that birds will guide souls to the place of the dead."

I say, "Like to heaven?"

Calvin says, "Yes. Heaven or whatever comes next."

I am thinking about the times when shafts of light shine down through clouds. How Benny Kilmartin told me those were paths to heaven. Funny thing. Well. Not funny. But if I could talk to Benny again, he would be able to tell about it. He would know for sure if that's a true thing, because if heaven is real, he has gone there.

Calvin kneels. Tucks himself down low to the floor.

He goes back to work on his dead man. I sink my fingers into Moonie's furry coat and he leans on me. So I scratch him. I sit back against the wall. I look at the aurochs. I move my head left and right. Funny thing. Sometimes the holy cow looks like he is moving.

chapter 43

ROCKS AND WORDS
AND GLITTER

Calvin and I get to the SWOOF at the same time. We get stuck in the doorway together. Pretty much on purpose. We pretend to be jammed there. Then we burst through. Calvin dives flat on his front onto the big couch. Disappears into the cushions. He looks like nothing but a backpack that got thrown down there. Makes me laugh when he sits up again. White hair all standing on end.

We hear Ms. Blinny come around the bookcase. She says, "Hi, Calvin! Hi, Mason! Did you bring your lunches like we planned?" She is waving to us. Hands full. She's got a flat round rock in one and a little jar of glitter dots in the other. Her fingers look gluey. Then, all of a sudden, she does *not* have that jar anymore.

She says, "Oh dear! Dropped it!"

Don't you know, Ms. Blinny has had herself another sparkle spill. This one has gone all across the small wooly rug.

Calvin and I help. We get down there and Calvin brings an index card. We scrape tiny dots back into the jar. We do okay. But a lot goes into the shaggy rug. A lot sticks to my hands. I try to wipe the dots off. But they spread all over me. That is how it happens when you are a sweaty gross-out of a kid.

Ms. Blinny tries her mini-vac on that rug. The glitter dots hang on tight to the rug hairs. I have a thought: Why does glitter need glue?

Calvin has the idea to take the rug outside and shake it. And Ms. Blinny says she will be grateful if we do.

So then I am at one end of the rug with Calvin at the other. We stand on the strip of grass at the front of the school. We shake the rug and the dots fly up. I am trying to do two things: One is shake the rug good and hard. One is go easy on Calvin. Don't want to fling him off into the parking lot. It goes okay. Calvin holds tight. The dots fly away on the wind.

Back inside, we wash our hands. Then we squeeze two chairs in. We sit by Ms. Blinny's desk and open up our lunches. She goes back to her project. There is a *Merrimack Gazette* spread open to cover the top of her desk so she won't get mess on it. She has lots of the smooth, flat rocks. They have words on them. Silver shiny Sharpie pen. Ms. Blinny has made the letters. Fancy. I try to read the words. Just to myself. But I can't.

She dabs glue all around the edge of one rock. Then she wipes the extra onto that *Merrimack Gazette*. Tell you what. That sticks to her finger. I think this: Newspaper on the desk is a very good idea for Ms. Blinny.

I go to take a bite of my sandwich. Find a little blue glitter dot on my bread. I try to pick it off. Not sure where that ends up. Could be I will eat a blue dot today. Well, the sandwich is good. Leftover roast chicken.

I swallow a bite. Use my napkin. I tell Calvin and Ms. Blinny, "Funny thing. Any sandwich I eat in the SWOOF tastes better than if I eat it in the cafeteria."

Ms. Blinny smiles a gentle sort of smile.

Calvin says, "Well, there are several reasons for that. The cafeteria is anything but a pleasant dining environment. It's loud, overcrowded, and likely to be hostile."

I like how Calvin Chumsky nails things on the head.

Ms. Blinny says, "Hmm. Yes. Cafeterias can be isolating. It's always best to dine with a friend. And you're right about the crowding. Merrimack has to catch up to itself. This town is full!" She spreads her arms wide. I keep one eye on that rock in her fingers. She says, "Our growing population means we will need to grow the schools, too."

I think about that. I wonder this: If Uncle Drum had

not sold some of our land for lots, where would the new houses be?

Ms. Blinny holds the glitter rock for us to see. She says, "What do you think, guys?"

I lean up to see the rock. Calvin too. I try again to read the words.

Calvin says, "It's nice. But what's it for? Why *courageous*?" Then Calvin reads more rocks. "Why *capable* and *respected*? Why *gentle*?" He says, "Why all the character-trait words?"

Ms. Blinny says, "Traits! Exactly. See, it's hard to identify the great qualities that we each possess. I'm all about helping you discover yours so you will believe in yourselves. That's what the SWOOF is here for. So, I'm making the rocks as reminders. Or keepsakes. Something you can hold in your hand and read over and over again."

I think this: Even a kid like me can do that. Remember one word off a rock. I say, "It's nice of you, Ms. Blinny. Real nice." Then I think this: If I hold one of those rocks I will be covered in colored glitter dots. Sweat is stronger than glue. But I do not say it.

Then Calvin starts talking. Might be about the rocks. Not sure. Because I have got a distraction. I'm trying to read a rock. It's the only one that does not have just one long word on it. It is three short ones. I get two words. Pretty sure I'm right. *Full* and *of*. Next I see the G, R, and A. I say it: "Full . . . of . . . *grass?*"

Calvin makes a small noise. Tries to keep it in behind that sandwich he is holding in his kitten paws. But I hear it.

Ms. Blinny says, "*Grace!*" She picks up the rock. Shows it to us. She says, "Full of grace. Hmm. Could have just been *graceful*, I guess." Now I know why Calvin made that noise. *Grass* instead of *grace* is pretty funny. Ms. Blinny says, "Oh my gosh! What if you *were* full of grass?"

I say, "Holy cow!"

Her eyes open wide. So does her smile. Calvin's too. All three of us crack up.

Then I say, "You know what? I did eat kind of a lot of grass one time."

Calvin says, "Yeah. That was last week, right? I saw you do that."

I nudge him. Not hard. I say, "When I was little!"

Ms. Blinny says, "I did that too!" She rubs glue off her fingers. She says, "High five, Mason!" We slap. She says, "And worse, I ate *mushrooms* one time in the sand box with my little brother. Boy! Never do that! We had to go to the hospital. They made us throw up."

Calvin says, "*Bluh-uhhh-uh.*" Rolls his eyes.

Ms. Blinny says, "Oh! Sorry, Calvin! Sorry!"

Calvin looks at the tail end of his sandwich. He maybe isn't going to finish that now. Sorry for him. But I laugh because Ms. Blinny is not afraid to be a gross-out.

When my sandwich is gone I stand up. I ball up my

lunch-bag trash in my hands. Paper and sweat. I look at the set of rocks on top of the newspaper. Glitter and glue are drying. That's when I see Benny Kilmartin. His picture. It is right on that page of that *Merrimack Gazette*. Right there on Ms. Blinny's desk.

I am not thinking. I am just saying, "Hey. Oh. Hey! That's Benny. Why is his picture there? What is that about?" I look at Ms. Blinny. She looks down at the picture.

She says, "Oh, Mason. *Your friend.* I'm sorry. The paper was just to keep my desk clean. I didn't even realize." Her cheeks turn red.

Calvin's feet bump Ms. Blinny's desk. He stands up to look. But mostly I see him looking at me.

I point to the page. I say, "This is him, Calvin. This is Benny Kilmartin. He wrote the acrostic poem. The one in my room. You remember?"

Calvin says, "Yes."

I look at Ms. Blinny. I say, "But why? Why is Benny's picture in the newspaper now? What is it about?"

Ms. Blinny says, "Well, this paper is from a while ago."

I say, "Like from when he died?"

Then Calvin answers. He says, "No. This is a few weeks old."

I am surprised he knows that.

Ms. Blinny says, "Well, stories about Benny run periodically because they are still trying to find out what happened. You know."

I say, "Oh yeah, I know. Because. Well. Lieutenant Baird. He says it's an investigation."

She says, "Yes."

I say, "Boy, I didn't know it was in the newspaper. We get the *Merrimack Gazette*. But Uncle Drum recycles pretty quick these days. And I can't read a newspaper anyway. But I guess it makes sense. Even if the news is sad it still goes in the paper."

I lean there a long time at Ms. Blinny's desk. I'm looking at Benny. It is the smiling picture. His two front teeth are squares. Pretty perfect ones. I forgot that about him. Somehow. And the forgetting comes up on me weird. Makes me wish I had not eaten all of my sandwich.

Calvin says, "Could Mason have the picture, Ms. Blinny?" Then he checks with me and says, "Do you want it?" Then back to Ms. Blinny he says, "Could we cut it out?"

She says, "Sure! If you don't mind a little glue and glitter with it."

I sure don't. So there is Ms. Blinny sliding rocks to one side. She grabs her scissors. She makes clean quick cuts while I dry my hands on my pants. I take the picture of my old friend, Benny Kilmartin. I hold it close to my eyes. I think this: I want to *see him* and *see him* and *see him*.

Got a feeling inside me. The loving memory of Benny.

chapter 44

DISTRESSED

So it is a Wednesday and it's good. On Wednesdays Calvin and I can get off at the cluster stop in peace and quiet. The lacrosse boys are at the school instead of playing in the Drinker yard. We scuff our feet because we have time to. I listen to the gravel swish and crunch. We walk into the crumbledown. Easy.

Inside, we have the banana shakes. Grandma folds laundry across the counter. We talk about our day. Just some. She likes to hear about school. Not just my part. Not just Calvin's part. She asks about her part too. Her old part. The job she used to have. She says, "Who's helping the special needs kids there these days?"

We tell her how there's a Mr. Tott and a Mrs. Sardello.

Both new. Sometimes one of them comes to the SWOOF with Annalissetta Yang. But just to drop her off. Other kids too. Grandma sighs a little like she is thinking back to her working days at the school.

But Calvin and I don't know more to tell her. We don't know all the new names. Merrimack Middle School has been adding grown-ups. Teachers and aides. You name it.

Of course, Shayleen comes out of my old room to be annoying. She says, "Has anybody seen Drum yet?" She is watching for him to come back from his day at the diner. She says, "I hope he's going to get here on time." She taps her teeth with her thumbnail. She paces.

Grandma says, "Is this about the Denim Show, Shayleen? Another shopping channel event? Drum already said no to that, sweetie."

Shayleen gets upset. And you can tell it is a two- or three-times-over kind of upset. She says something about how she just wants a jacket. A faded thing. With fraying threads here and there. "*Distressed,*" she says, and I think that sounds like the jacket is pretty sad.

I ask her, "Why do you need that? You don't go outside. Except to stand on the porch and watch me bring boxes from the UPS truck. And Shayleen, if you want a holey jacket, I could drag the one you have on behind the tractor. I'll run it over for you too."

Calvin about loses his banana milkshake out his nose. I see Grandma making smiling minnow eyes at us.

Calvin gulps down a laugh. He says, "Mason . . . don't pick on her."

I say, "I wasn't picking!" Because I really wasn't. I say, "I'm trying to help!" Because I really was. This time.

Now he laughs into his elbow like he doesn't want Shayleen to see. Doesn't want to hurt her feelings.

Shayleen laughs too. But it's squeaky. Whiny. Like it will turn to crying. She goes to the front window of the crumbledown to look for Drum. This is how it goes with her. She will try one more time to get that sorry jacket. And Uncle Drum will have a hard time saying no. He might even say yes.

Truth is, I feel bad for Shayleen. Not about the jacket, but about how she doesn't get happier even when she gets to buy. Well, no. She does. But it's only at first when she makes the order. And then some more when the UPS truck comes. But in the end the things don't fill her up. Tell you what. She has not missed her big plastic salad chiller bowl one bit. Even that makes me feel bad for her.

I think this: Shayleen is distressed.

So I say, "Sorry, Shayleen. I really wasn't teasing. I know I do it some. But today, I didn't mean it." Then she gives me a teary nod. Then all I want to do is get out of there.

So we do that.

chapter 45

WEDNESDAY MODE

Calvin and I skip the root cellar today. We are free to be visible. Calvin calls this Wednesday mode. And he calls it the aboveground part of our lives. Makes me laugh because it is true. I have noticed that quite a lot of times. True things are funny.

We go walking out through the rows of apple trees. Calvin brings his backpack in case we stay out until suppertime. We might. Tell you what. The aurochs and the dead man and the Caves of Lascaux are awesome. But I like being in the orchard. I like seeing the parts we still own. Even if there is a big waste of apples on the ground. We step around where the bees come to drink.

I tell Calvin, "Did you know that you have to listen for the insects?"

He says, "Really? What's that about?"

I say, "Well, you have your good insects and your bad ones. And you want to keep your spraying down. Or not at all."

He says, "Oh, you mean pesticides?"

I say, "Yep. The Buttles don't like them. Been careful about them from way back. And sometimes that cost us some of the crop. But my grandpa said it plenty of times. My uncle Drum too. You have to think about the bigger picture. The health of that orchard."

Calvin says, "Right. There must be a lot to know."

My brain has filled up. Feels like all these things I know about being an orchard family have moved up front right where I can remember them. I could talk a blue streak about apples. But not so sure Calvin wants to hear all of that. So I show him just one more thing.

I say, "Look at that. The Winesaps and Macouns are ripe. But up at the other end of the orchard, the Paula Reds? Done. The apple season stretches pretty nice and long if you have enough varieties."

Then I reach. Bring a branch low. I'm careful. I know how to do it. I tell Calvin, "Go on and pick. Twist of the wrist." Calvin picks two apples. I let the branch go back up. Then I tug up my pants. Something is going on with those. Been slipping down lately.

Calvin hands me one apple. Bites into the other. He says, "So that farm stand out by the road, that was where you sold them?"

I say, "Oh yeah. Sold plenty there. Pies and apple butter too. And we had PYO. Pick Your Own. And there was the company that came for the cider apples. The McIntoshes and Empires mostly."

Calvin says, "Couldn't they do it again? Like, bring back the Buttle orchard?"

I hear that word *they*. I guess he means Uncle Drum and Grandma. They are the adults. I tell Calvin, "Don't you know I wish for it. I think there's something about that. Our hard times, I mean. It was six years ago now. That's pretty hard for me to remember. But two funerals right together is a double punch. Everyone dropped off what they were doing. My grandma gave up her teacher's aide job at the school. She quit baking too. Just too sad to get it all done. I guess. And then two bad crops in the orchard and I think that put Uncle Drum off trying. He never got going again."

Calvin says, "Are they still too sad now?"

I think about that. I say, "Grandma is kind of better. She calls that kitchen her first big step. The way she keeps it nice now. Before that she had to set her alarm for mornings. Stop herself from sleeping past the sun. She gets on my uncle Drum. Tells him he needs to take a step too. If

I were him, I would call that cider company. Tell you why. Even when you don't have the prettiest apples, you can still make good cider. And they come get them."

Calvin says, "Yeah? So? Maybe suggest it. Have you?"

I say, "Oh yeah. He tells me maybe. Then he tells me never mind."

We eat our apples. I toss my core as far as I can. And who comes running to bring that back to me? Moonie Drinker. He bounds through the tall grass. I stoop to catch him, but then I let him plow me down. He stands on my chest and licks my face. Calvin and I laugh. Then Moonie sits half on me, half off, and eats that apple core. Whole thing. I know he's not supposed to be out of the Drinker yard. I don't know how that happens. But I cannot help it. I love to see this dog.

We hike down to the small pond. This is the bottom of the hill away from the new neighborhood. Marks the end of the orchard. Calvin and I sit. He leans back on his backpack. Moonie goes around the pond. Nose to the grass all the way like that's his job. A bug flies up out of the weeds. Makes him jump off all four feet. Then he tries to snap it out of the air. Calvin and I laugh so hard.

I pull that photo of Benny Kilmartin out of my pocket. Good thing is, Ms. Blinny put some clear contact paper on it. That was Calvin's idea. I would have ruined it by now. The way I keep bringing it out to look at it. My fingers, my sweat.

I tell Calvin, "Wish I could see all the words that went with this picture. Even though I couldn't read them all."

Calvin says, "I read it."

I say, "Really? You did?"

Calvin says, "Well, yeah. Stuff comes up on my tablet on the local newsfeed. Or I browse. That caught my eye mostly because of you, Mason. Once I knew Benny was your friend, and once I read his acrostic poem, I was interested. And also, well, it's kind of this big thing here in Merrimack. A hard story."

I say. "Yeah. Kids are not supposed to die. And a lot of people knew him. And miss him. Can you remember what it said? In the paper?"

Calvin nods. He says, "It told what happened. There were parts about the police asking questions. How they think one, or more than one, person might know things they are not saying. They want help and cooperation. They want people to come forward with information."

I say, "That . . . that sounds . . . I don't know. *Disturbing.* Sounds like they think someone has a secret. Dark one." I twitch a bit when I say it. I switch the photo hand to hand. Dry my palms on my pants. I look at a blue glitter dot that got stuck under the contact paper. Next to Benny's ear. Wonder if it's the dot I thought I ate.

I tell Calvin, "Lieutenant Baird says he wants *my* cooperation. I try to tell him everything I know. But like I told you, he interrupts. Like he wants to hear something different from what I have to say. I don't know what. Maybe some of those parts I wrote with the Dragon will help him."

Calvin runs his hands through the grass. He nods his head. I see him close one eye in the low sun. He says, "I think they want to know more about the place where it happened."

"Where Benny died? Like, about the tree fort?"

Calvin shrugs. He says, "You could say that. The article mentioned an address. It said at 1054 Swaggertown Road. Then it said town records show the property is an orchard owned by Janette Buttle."

I say, "See, that's my grandma. She is Janette."

Calvin says, "It says Benny fell from a ladder on that property and that a playmate of Benny's found him."

I say, "Me. I'm the one. Holy cow. It's in the paper?"

Calvin nods.

I say, "See, and I keep thinking, isn't that all there is? He fell. In some way that hurt him real bad. Isn't that what happened? The lieutenant thinks there is more to know. But I keep thinking he might be done with the puzzle. Because what more could there be?"

Calvin shakes his head. He is very quiet now. We both watch Moonie coming full circle around the pond. I say, "So the Buttles are in the newspaper too. We are in there with Benny."

Calvin looks up. Pulls his lips in. He nods. For just one second I think I see it. He looks sad to see me.

chapter 46

RUN, SPLIT, RUN

We are still by the pond—Calvin, Moonie, and me. We're all lying back in the grass. The dog is belly up. Calvin is watching the sky. It's the kind of day you lose track, but I know it's getting near to suppertime. Low sun. Cool air. And my *growling* belly. Calvin hears it.

He says, "Are you hungry, Mason?"

I say, "Yeah. But I like waiting it out as long as I can. Not letting the day be over with."

Calvin says, "I get that. And you know what else is a drag? Having to be home earlier and earlier. To make it in before dark."

I say, "Right. We are getting shorter days."

Then we hear a yell. A *whoop*. Comes from the edge of

the orchard. Moonie rolls onto his feet. Ears up.

Then we hear this: "Buttle! Chumsky! We're coming to *own* you!" Matt and Lance march out of the tall grass across the pond. Lacrosse sticks up and loaded. They waggle them at us. Moonie steps left. Then right. Then stands with one foot up.

Calvin says, "Ugh! This is an ambush."

We both scramble up off the ground.

He says, "So much for Wednesday mode!"

We are on our feet. Backing up. Matt and Lance are coming around the pond. Heading straight for us. The first apple sails in. Plunks into the water. We are off and running, with Moonie Drinker coming along beside. He is faster than all of us. That dog could be home in a split. But he stays close.

The going is tough unless you are a bounding dog. The tall grass is a tripping thing. Gets wrapped on the shoes. Calvin grunts when an apple hits him. I put him to the front of me. Wish he didn't have the backpack on. Calvin is not the best runner. But we go—heading for the crumbledown. Still out of sight. Still far up the hill.

I look behind.

They are gaining. Not good! We are going to get *applesauced*.

Calvin shouts to me. He says, "Split up! We'll circle! I'll meet you. You know where! *Don't give it up, Mason!*"

He goes up. Left. I go down. Right. Moonie comes

with me. I worry. What if Matt and Lance both go after Calvin? Can't let it happen.

I stop and turn. Stand in the path. I raise my arms, waggle my hands, and stamp my feet at them. Out of the corner of my eye I see a flash of white. Calvin's hair. Then his backpack. He is pushing his way up the hill.

I flap my arms and caw at Matt and Lance. In comes an apple. And I can't believe it—I catch it! I whip it back at them. Then turn and run. Moonie follows.

Apples whiz by my head. Splat on my back. I run down the orchard rows. Not so sure where Calvin is now. I think of his tan-sandy shoes slapping down. Backpack swinging. How he is not so good at running.

Moonie is galloping beside me. I look back. I see Matt. Close. And Lance. Not as close. Good thing is, they are both chasing *me*. Not Calvin. But I wonder how in heck I'm going to circle back up.

An apple smacks Moonie. He skitters sideways. Matt aims at him again. I try to send Moonie ahead but he doesn't understand. I about fall over him. I have to run on. I weave through the tree trunks all along the row. Matt is totally on me.

My breath is out. I slow down. Then I stop. Behind a tree. I have to. I'm breathing like a beast. I want to head uphill. To the crumbledown. Moonie waits. Looks up to me. Brown-gold eyes. He wants to know, *What's next?*

Shower of apples is what. Man! They *cream* me! Apples

smack me and the trees with a *whap-whap* sound. Juice sprays. Pulp flies. Matt and Lance have scooped some soft ones. They reach low with their sticks and reload. Easy to do. So many apples, ripe and dropped.

I decide. There is no getting to the crumbledown now. So I turn the chase. Head for the Drinker house. I think this: If I get Moonie home this will end. He races next to me. I tug up on my pants. Jump the clumps of tall grasses. I keep running. I get close enough to see down the hill into the Drinkers' yard. *Someone* is there. Looking up. Hand shading his eyes.

Corey McSpirit. He sees me coming.

I hear him call, "What's going on? Where is everyone?"

I think this: What does he mean? Can't he *see*?

I look behind me.

What?

No Matt. No Lance.

I stop there on the hill. Between the crumbledown and the Drinker house. I rest. Hands on knees. Breathe in and out. Moonie waits at my feet. Pink tongue hanging. I wipe my face on my shirt.

I lift my head and look through the rows of trees. Where did they go? And what about Calvin? I feel a few seconds press by. Thud of my heart going with them. I see our tractor sitting in the dip. Wall of thorns behind it. And I know the root cellar door is behind the thorns. I think this: Calvin made it. Bet he is there with his eye to the knothole. I start toward it. Just slow. No point in running. So I walk. But then Moonie darts ahead—way ahead. And don't you know it, he is heading for the root cellar door.

I think, no, no, no! Corey McSpirit is watching! Moonie, *don't give up the root cellar!*

I call, "Hey! Moonie! Moonie!" Tricky thing. I don't want to be too loud about it. Don't want to call attention. But then Moonie goes on by the door. He heads up top. Stands in the brambles. Stops with one paw up the way he does. Good boy!

Then I hear a yell from down the hill. It's Corey McSpirit. He hollers, *"Run!"*

I stand still, wondering, does he mean me? Then don't you know it. Matt and Lance come from around the front of the crumbledown. Sticks in the air. Eyes on me.

Matt yells, "Lost the pygmy! Get the Sweat Head!" Lance comes with him. Both barreling down the hill. Both waving sticks at me.

I can't get by them. Can't get home. And now here comes Moonie again. Fast as can be. I take off. He stays at my heels. This is it. My last run. I keep my sights on Corey McSpirit down by the Drinker doorway. He is the finish line. He calls to Matt and Lance behind me.

He says, "Hey! You guys! Come on. Give it up!"

But they don't. And they are gaining. Then Matt swings his stick low. Takes a swat at his dog.

I pick up Moonie—on the run. And it's like that dog

knows to curl up and hook his paws. Like he's holding on to me. It is not so easy to run with a dog in your arms. And it's not like Moonie is so tiny. I just have to get him to the door. Get him to Mrs. Drinker. I don't want to get Matt in trouble. Don't care about that. But I do care about this dog.

I am there. Just outside the house. I make wide eyes at Corey. He watches. I try to be steady. Try to make my voice sound easy. Like I am not really breathing hard. Even though I am. Totally.

I call, "Mrs. Drinker! Hey, Mrs. Drinker!" I see the back door crack open. I say, "Brought Moonie ba—"

BAM!

Matt's whole body hits my whole body. He leads with that lacrosse stick going sideways. I lose my hold on Moonie. He slips to the ground. I am *bashed* smack into the side of the Drinker house. A big grunt comes out of me. A pain shoots up my elbow. Good thing is, I see Moonie scoot away. Just fine.

Corey McSpirit says, "*Matt!* Are you kidding me? What was that for?"

Now Mrs. Drinker is on the step.

She says, "Matty! Whoa! Whoa! Did I really just see that? You *rammed* Mason right into the side of the house. What were you thinking?"

Matt is red in the face. Huffing and puffing. Guess I did give him a good chase. He points the lacrosse stick at me. He screams. He says, "Buttle had our dog again! He steals him!" Matt spits on the ground. Pretty close to my feet. He says, "He takes him! All the time!"

I have to say it. I tell Mrs. Drinker, "I don't steal your dog. I wouldn't do that. He just comes around, is all."

Matt says, "Yeah, well if he does it's because he likes rats and skunks. Like the ones living under your ugly house, Sweat Head."

Mrs. Drinker says, "Matty! Enough!"

She turns to me. She says, "Mason, honey, are you all right?"

I cup my elbow. Open and close tingling fingers. I say, "Yeah. I think I'm pretty okay." I try to smile about it. But tell you what. That was a big hit.

Mrs. Drinker looks me over to see if I am okay. But I look at her house to see if I put a dent in it. Looks all right.

Most important thing is this: Moonie is right close beside Mrs. Drinker now. She puts a hand on his head. He wags. Safe and sound.

She says, "I know Moonie gets loose. He loves to run."

I think this: Well, he sure has been running today.

Then I say, "He just comes over because he knows me. From the times I take care of him. That's all."

Mrs. Drinker nods her head. She says, "I know. And that's fine." Then she faces Matt. Straight on. She says, "But Matty, it's *not* fine that you crash into Mason like you just did. And the name-calling and insults? That's unacceptable. You need to apologize."

He won't. I know he won't. He looks up into the air. Puts his lips tight. And the waiting makes me squirm. I wish she had not bothered with this. Then Matt starts humming.

Mrs. Drinker says, "Okay. Matty. Inside. Now." She points. As if he doesn't know the way.

Matt says, "No! We hardly got to practice at all. We're still going to take accuracy shots."

I think this: His shots are pretty accurate. I am covered in apple mush. Kind of wonder if Mrs. Drinker sees that.

She shakes her head at Matt. She says, "No. Not this time." She looks up at Lance and Corey. She says, "Boys, I'm sorry, you'll have to go home now. It's going to be suppertime for everyone soon anyway."

I'll tell you something about Mrs. Drinker. She looks worn out about all of this. Even more when Matt pushes by her to get inside. He rams her too. Not like he did to me. But some.

Lance is slow about leaving. Corey McSpirit tells him, "Come on. We gotta go. Get your stuff."

They head away. Lance does not show me his middle finger. Not today. Not with Mrs. Drinker still close to the door. But funny thing, Corey McSpirit turns around and raises a hand like a wave. And he lifts his chin. *At me.*

And I can't help thinking it again. There is something about Corey McSpirit. He's not the same as Matt and Lance. He's nicer. But it's more than that. He seems sorry about them being the way they are. I can see it on his face.

chapter 47

SUPPER CALL

I climb the hill for home. Legs ache. This has been a long Wednesday. Some good. Some bad. Some I don't have figured out. Like what happened up here around the crumbledown. With Matt and Lance. One of them said it: *Lost the pygmy!* That's Calvin, of course. I smile about it. Wonder how he gave them the slip. I know he will tell me. I know where to find him. I can kind of feel his eye on me.

I look over my shoulder. Make sure the coast is clear. Nobody left in the Drinker yard. I slip behind the tractor. Reach into the brambles and pull the rope to open the door.

I step down in. I pull the door shut. Start talking into

the dark. I say, "Calvin! Holy cow! How did you get back here . . . so . . . fast? Calvin? *Hey, Calvin?*"

I stand still. The root cellar is way dark. And silent.

I reach back. Push the door a crack for light. But it doesn't really help. I blink. A few times. I look around again.

Calvin is not here.

My eyes adjust. Enough so I can see the shape of the great aurochs on the pale wall. Strong and mighty. I say, "Have you seen him?"

It's a joke with no one to hear it. I stare at the beast and it happens again. Looks like he is moving. Can almost hear him breathing. A whispering kind of in and out. I think, what if that aurochs could run right off that wall? Out the door and into the orchard. My brain makes it up. Quick thought. Then it's gone.

My stomach growls—out loud—in the quiet root cellar. Makes a noise like a groan or a moo. I am as hungry as an aurochs. Makes me laugh. Bet Calvin got hungry too. Went on home for supper. Before dark. That's the rule. I think, darn! I want to hear how he made his getaway. The telling will have to wait for tomorrow. I pull the door shut. I make sure the bramble blanket covers it up right. The camouflage.

I come up from the dip in the backyard thinking about Matt and his mom. Ugly scene, that was. Makes me sorry for her. And I'm kind of sorry for Corey McSpirit too.

I catch a whiff of myself. It's sour apples. And armpits. And something else too. I smell like the side of the Drinkers' house. Now that is something I never thought had much smell. But getting rammed into a place will make you notice. My elbow still aches. Good scrape on it too.

Coming around to the front of the crumbledown, there's another smell. Bacon and maple. Uncle Drum slides out of his truck. Sun is down. Wonder if he's just getting back from the diner. Drinking coffee right up to suppertime. There's a long, long Wednesday for you.

He waits for me at the porch. He says, "Hey, Mason. You okay? Looks like you need a fresh shirt."

I say, "Yeah. Well. That's pretty much always."

Uncle Drum laughs. Just a grunt. He says, "Where's Calvin today?"

I say, "He was here. But he went home." I jab my thumb toward Jonagold Path.

Uncle Drum says, "Sorry I missed him."

I almost say it. If Uncle Drum wanted to see Calvin maybe he should not have sat so long at the diner. But I don't say it. No point.

Inside the crumbledown I smell Italian sausages—and it is *so* good. That is the kind of smell you want to end your day with. Juicy. Salty.

Shayleen is putting napkins around the table in a slap-down sort of way. She's having a pout. Must be the Denim Show didn't work out so well. Must be she didn't get to order her new jacket. The distressed.

I go on up, change my shirt. Bad thing is, it is my last clean one. Must be a dozen dirty ones on the floor. My own fault. I have been too *now and then* about this. I gather them up and dump them down the chute. Smell of sausages comes up through. Grandma is going to see my shirts land in the basket there at the end of the kitchen. It will be up to her if I have clean ones for tomorrow.

We sit down to eat. Noodles and cheese with sausage on the side. All through supper Shayleen keeps looking at Uncle Drum then making a droopy face. He won't look back. She eats her food. Baby bites. Not me. I dig in. I do some real eating.

Phone rings. We all stay put. Let the machine pick it up. It will be one of those calls nobody wants. Something recorded. Like the cardholder services one from that lady named Rachel. Or the guy called Kevin with a power washer. Or the offer for a cheap price on a cruise. Like any Buttles would get up and go on one of those.

But it's not any of those. We hear Margie. Margie who works at the Chumsky house. She says hello. She might be a little mad or something. She says she is calling for Calvin. Or, *about* Calvin. We listen. She talks like Calvin is not there. I don't get that.

It happens that I stop still and look at Shayleen while I am forking noodles into my mouth. She says, "Ew, Mason! That's gross! And dry off!" She pushes the roll of paper towels at me. I miss some of Margie's call.

Grandma gets up. She stands by the phone. Brow wrinkled up. Margie is still talking. She says something about when the Chumsky parents get home. She says, "So I'd appreciate it if you'd give me a call back in the next few minutes. Please." The call ends.

Grandma looks at me. She says, "Calvin went home, didn't he?"

I nod yes. I have a cheek full of sausage. I try not to talk with my mouth full. Don't want to stir up Shayleen.

Grandma picks up the phone. She dials Margie back. She talks. Then she listens. We all wait. Grandma tucks the phone under her chin. She says, "Mason. Where did you last see Calvin?"

I think about it. I remember him going to the left. And up. Scrambling. His white hair. The backpack swinging.

Grandma says, "Mason? Where?"

I say, "It was a ways down the orchard. He was running up the hill. To come here."

Grandma looks at me. Really *at me*. She says, "And when was that? Do you know what time?"

I shake my head. I think this: The sun was low. The air was cool. . . .

She says, "But were you with him?"

I say, "I was. But then, not. I was going to meet him again. But some stuff happened. I was gone kind of long taking the dog back down to the Drinkers. So Calvin went on home. To supper."

Grandma shakes her head at me. Face full of worry. She says, "No, honey. He didn't. He's *not* there."

I push back my chair. Stand right up. I go out the door of the crumbledown. Daylight is gone. Has been for a while now. I cross Swaggertown. Head up Jonagold Path. I call for Calvin. No answer.

I turn and look back toward the crumbledown. See Uncle Drum come off the porch with the flashlight. He's moving at a trot. Fast as I have seen him go anywhere in a long time. Looks like he will circle our place.

I go on. Up into the yards of all the new houses. I call Calvin's name again and again. Tell you what, every time I do not find him I feel the world tip. Little more. Little more.

I am almost to the Chumskys' place when a police car goes by me. Merrimack Pee Dee. I watch the cruiser turn into Calvin's driveway.

The world goes upside down.

chapter 48

THE SEARCH FOR
CALVIN CHUMSKY

Everybody searches. Everybody phones everybody else. It's after dark. Calvin should be home.

I stand out front at the crumbledown. Sent home. The searchers are here. They want grown-ups only now. I watch the flashlight beams sweep through the yards up on Jonagold Path. So many. A picture of Calvin goes to every house. Happens fast. And people come out to call, *"Calvin! Calvin!"*

On my own I check out in front of our place. Seems like that's where Matt and Lance came from when they said they lost the pygmy. I want to look fast—find him fast. But I make myself be slow and careful. I look behind our branchy shrubs. Could be he hid here. But this doesn't make sense. It is not like Calvin would need to stay hidden so long.

Shayleen has her head out her window when I come by. Elbows on the sill. She is biting her thumb. She says, "Is there any sign of him, Mason?" She sniffles. She is crying. I know it's for real. Nobody ever said it. But Shayleen likes Calvin.

I shake my head at her. I say, "No luck yet. Still looking."

I walk along our rickety porch. Past the mousey chair. I wrap my arm around the porch post. Look out to all the near places where I wish I would see Calvin right now. I grit my teeth.

What happens is this: You just cannot stand it. It is too much like another time. When another friend did not go home for supper. The worry is the most giant kind. I see the mud-green. It's all in patches. Got a feeling. Like my heart leaking into my chest.

Then I think this: What if I was wrong? What if Calvin circled wider for that chase? What if he got to the root cellar *after* me? There is not much of me that believes it. No way he would wait there all through suppertime. And up to now.

But I go. I slip back down to the dip in the yard. Tuck myself behind the tractor. No one is watching me. They are looking for Calvin out in the dark. I fumble for the rope with the knot in it. The thorns bite my hands. But I make it inside. And don't you know, it is even darker in the root cellar. And no flashlight. Uncle Drum took that to go searching with the others.

I cannot see. So I don't try to. I close my eyes. I walk my hands all along the painted stony walls. I am quick, but I am careful. I feel the wall where I drew with charcoal. I feel the bump of the aurochs's rump. Smell the oil crayons. I know this whole place. I touch all the walls. Then I touch all the air. Every bit of it. Arms out in front of me. I get low. I brush my hands along the floor. My fingers hit something soft and lumpy. I about jump out of my skin.

But it is not Calvin. It's the rug that Moonie likes. I creep along. Bump my forehead into the bench we made with the five-gallon buckets. This whole time, I whisper Calvin's name. I hope and I hope. I check every inch of that root cellar.

But I find just what I think I will find. Nothing. I sit back on my heels. I whisper, "Calvin, where can you be?" Then I whisper, "Calvin, do you know where you are? *Tell me.*"

Then I remember how it was to find Benny Kilmartin at the bottom of the tree house. I think, no, Mason. Don't think like that. It's Calvin now. Find Calvin.

I get up and go outside where I can see. Strange thing, that is. The root cellar being darker than the night. I close the door and that blanket of brambles behind me.

Some searchers come down across Swaggertown Road. Giant fireflies. They bob through the cluster stop. Down

McIntosh Circle to the new neighborhood below us. Some head into the space in the middle—our orchard. I want to go with them. I don't need a light. I can see without.

I think this: All of us need to check every mound of grass and make sure none of those is Calvin. We have to look up every tree. Even though Calvin is not a climber. Check anyway. So I start marching out there.

I don't get far. Uncle Drum calls for me. I turn around. See him up at the crumbledown. Looking down off the end of the porch. And I see the shape of someone else beside him.

Lieutenant Baird.

chapter 49

THE LAST TO SEE

Don't you know, the lieutenant wants to have a talk with me.

We go inside. Sit at the table. No notebook tonight. And Grandma does not wipe down the kitchen. She and Uncle Drum stand near me. Shayleen has her eye at the crack of the bedroom door. The lieutenant is jittery. He talks fast.

What we get to is this: I am the last to see Calvin. Makes me sound special but not special. And I try to think, is it true? Am I the last? Do we know? But I think the lieutenant will not want to hear me ask it.

He thumps a finger on the table. He says, "Mason, this is very serious. You understand?" I nod my head.

He says, "We have *a second missing boy*. And here we are. With you."

I swallow down on nothing. Dry air. I think about that worry I have. That I am bad luck. I say, "You mean second . . . like Benny Kilmartin was missing first? And now Calvin?"

He says, "Yes. Those are the two boys I'm referring to. I need you to tell me what happened today, Mason. Let's get to it."

I wipe my face on my shoulder. My thinking goes backward.

The lieutenant says, "I need to know everything. Was there a trick? A game?"

I say, "No. Just a chase. And then I lost him."

"You were chasing him?"

I say, "Not me."

"You just said you lost him."

"Yeah. But. No. No. I don't chase. But we were running. Both of us. Then we had to split up. Then it was suppertime. He ran home. I mean, I thought he did. Up Jonagold Path. But now . . ."

"Yes? Now what? What do you think now?"

I say, "Now he is missing and the others might have—"

"Who are the others?"

I take a breath. I am trying, trying to hold on to the sequence in my brain. But when the lieutenant interrupts

I have to go back. Catch the thing I was trying to say.

I say, "Oh. Umm. The others are the neighbor kids who—"

"And who are they?"

"Oh. Okay. That's Matt Drinker. Lance Pierson. They said they lost him. I think they meant he . . . disappeared."

"Disappeared?" Some spit flies with that P sound.

The lieutenant is not happy. I hear him breathing through his nose. Being impatiently patient. That's what that is. He will get madder. I know it. I reach for the paper towels. Tear one off the roll. Drag it down my face. I stop and hold it over my eyes.

The lieutenant says, "Mason, why were you heading into the orchard just now?"

I bring down the paper towel. I say, "To look for Calvin." I look at the lieutenant. Straight on. I say, "I'm just like everyone. I want him back."

The lieutenant says, "Then you help me, Mason!"

I try. I close my eyes. I start to see it, the chase. The map of it. It's a going-backward map. I try to think of telling a story. Sequence. But it is going backward, backward, backward.

So I say, "The *last* thing was, I dropped Moonie at the Drinker house. Their dog. And before that, I was in the orchard. Middle of the hill. I was looking up to the crumbledown. This house. I saw Matt and Lance. They said they lost Calvin. Before that, they were coming around the corner. Of the porch." I look at the lieutenant now. He lets a breath out. *At me.* I say, "Sorry. I don't know the part before. I mean, I don't know their map. Or Calvin's map. That piece is missing."

The lieutenant makes a note. He puts his hands on the table. Straightens his elbows. He says, "You can be sure that we will talk to those other boys."

Grandma says, "When? When will you interview them? It sounds like they—"

Now the lieutenant interrupts her. He says, "There is a process here. I will have someone speak to them. But this comes first. As far as we know, Mason is the last person to see Calvin Chumsky. But how about this, Mason? How about you walk me through this map of yours. But let's go frontward instead of backward. Can you do that? How about we begin from when you got off the bus here today?"

I say, "Oh. Okay."

"In fact, let's go *walk* that map. You take me, Mason." The lieutenant gets up. The table shakes. He says, "Let's go out there. Let's *retrace.*"

Uncle Drum says, "That will be the three of us." He flicks on his flashlight.

So we do that.

I think it is a good idea. Better than sitting and interrupting.

It starts with the cluster stop. It's Wednesday quiet. Two banana milkshakes. Then out of the crumbledown

with Calvin. Into the orchard paths. I walk. The lieutenant stays on my heels. The orchard is different at
night. The shadows. Dark fruits. Some clinging. Some
dropped. The sweep of the lieutenant's flashlight beside
me. We hike. I am pretty sure we reach the pond same way
Calvin and I did earlier this day.

Tell you what. The lieutenant is interested in that
pond. He says, "Any swimming?"

I say, "No. Too weedy. Too mucky. And besides this is
fall."

The lieutenant leads Uncle Drum and me. Walks all
the way around the pond. I tell him Calvin and I were
not on that other side. Just Matt and Lance were. I tell
him two times. He brings up the flashlight. Makes me
squint. He says, "Why don't you want me to walk around
this pond, Mason? Any reason why Calvin couldn't have
come back this way?"

I say, "I don't know."

Makes me feel stupid to say it. I feel stupid that I don't
really know what the lieutenant means.

We go around the pond. Find nothing. But the lieutenant calls for helpers. They come quick. He sends them
out around the pond.

I say, "There's more of the map. A part that comes
after the pond."

He says, "And you say Calvin was still with you?"

I say, "Yes."

He wonders if I am sure. But I am. He tells the searchers to stay with it. Stay at the pond. He tells me, "Okay, Mason. Let's go on."

So we do that.

On through the orchard. And then comes the hard part of the map. I say, "Calvin and I split up. Was near here. Not sure where."

The lieutenant points me at the orchard rows. The grasses. He watches my face. I can feel that. Sometimes he holds up the light. So he can see me. He says, "Think. Look and think."

Uncle Drum says, "He's doing it. Give him a chance."

I look up to the left and point. Finger moving. I say, "Calvin went up that way. On his own. But I don't know exactly where. But I went on—"

The lieutenant says, "I'll bet you can remember." He shines that light in my face. Then up that hill. He says, "Where, Mason?"

I scan. We are near it. Pretty sure. Near the place I saw Calvin go scrambling. I'm afraid to say it in case I am wrong. There is some part where the tall grass is flat down. A trail. We walk it even though it is not my map. The trail goes sort of toward the crumbledown. But it winds a bit. I tell the lieutenant, "You know, this path could be made by Calvin. Or by a deer. Or rabbits. It's hard to know."

Uncle Drum says, "You're right. Could be an animal path."

The trail dies away in the shorter grass now. But the lieutenant and Uncle Drum and I make a guess. We go up and across the front of the crumbledown. The lieutenant shines his light all along the stony foundation. In behind the shrubs.

I think this: Already looked here. Did that myself. But I don't say it.

We cross the porch. To the mousey chair. The lieutenant gives that a shove. Might be because he is mad. But then we see it. Calvin's backpack. Drops out from behind the chair.

My heart takes a hop. I say, "That's Calvin's! That's his!"

The lieutenant goes stony faced. He bounces his foot up and down on our cruddy porch boards. He eyes the steps. He says, "I want to have a look under this decking. Now."

It is Uncle Drum who does it. Starts kicking up the boards himself. They come up easy. If they don't he yanks on them. Bare hands. Or he kicks harder. I drag the mousey chair down the old steps. The lieutenant shines a light. Grandma and Shayleen hear the racket. They come watch from the window. We all call out.

"Calvin? *Calvin?*"

But Calvin is not beneath our porch. The joists sit there. Bare old bones with no skin on top. Everything is worse than a minute ago when we still thought we might find him.

Weather comes in. A downpour. Makes the search harder. Postponed, is what I hear.

I tell the lieutenant I can't postpone. I will go back to my map. Walk the orchard again. Rain doesn't bother me. Not as much as wondering where Calvin is. But he says no. He wants me in. He is firm about it.

Grandma wonders do I want the rest of my supper. Because I left my plate. But I can't eat. I climb the stairs. I kick off my shoes. Skip stuffing them with newspapers. I drop my pants in a heap. I don't really go to bed. I lie on top in my sweaty T-shirt. Stare up at the chestnut beams. I think this: The Buttle house won't sleep tonight.

And it doesn't. I know because I hear the washing machine filling. Later, it spins. Empties. Spins. Then the dryer flips clothes. My T-shirts. *Tink*-tink-a-tink. *Tink*-tink-a-tink.

I lie awake wondering where I would be if I could be Calvin. I hear the rain and hope he is dry. And safe. I think of the Chumsky parents. I wonder if I will see them in the morning. I wonder if they will wear sad-to-see-you faces. I think of the first missing boy. Benny, who believed that shafts of light make the path to heaven.

chapter 50

HOT RAIN

It might be that I have slept for a few minutes. Can see the darkest part of night just ending. I think about light and dark. I sit up. I suck a breath.

I *know* where Calvin is!

I scramble off the bed. Jump into my pants. I stuff my feet into my open shoes. I hurry. Laces flying. I thunder down the stairs. Hands barely on the rail. I snag the flashlight off the hook and swing the door open. I leap over the ruined porch. Then I run. Full out.

I round to the back of the house. Head for the dip. I call Calvin's name. My foot lands on something strange. Slippery. Hard and round. My legs go out from under. I go down on my side. The flashlight slams the hill. I can see in the beam. The plastic salad-bowl thing. The cap of the light shaft. It is sliding away. Down the wet hill. Like a saucer sled.

I scramble up. Hurry to the root cellar door. I reach into the thorns and haul it open. Inside, I stand below the Shaft of the Dead Man. All is dark. Too dark. I tip the flashlight up. Shine it into the shaft. What *am* I seeing? Is it anything?

I call, "Calvin! Calvin!"

Something comes down on me. Like hot rain. Stings my head. Drips down my shoulders and arms. There's a smell. Not so good. I step up on a bucket. I reach my arm up. Up into the Shaft of the Dead Man. *Something* fits in my palm. I grab it. Tug it. Pull it down. And there I am holding one tan-sandy shoe.

"Mason?"

"Calvin? *Calvin!*"

"Mason?"

"Calvin! Oh! Holy cow!"

He says, "I'm sorry . . ."

"What? What did you say?" I talk up into the shaft. "You're sorry?"

"Yeah . . . I just peed."

I think this: hot rain.

"But Calvin! It's *you!*"

He says, "Yeah. I'm hanging out . . . in the Shaft of the Dead Man."

He is hard to hear. He is raspy. Like he wants breath and can't get any. Like he wants to be funny. But this isn't.

I say, "Aw, Calvin! *How?* We searched for hours! And then—just now—I woke up and I knew where to find you! Don't know how. But I knew! But Calvin, I'm going to go get help. So you wait, okay? You wait."

He says, "I will. I have to. I'm stuck. It's *so* tight. And Mason, I'm not in great shape. You need to tell them. I can't stay awake . . . and . . . and . . ."

"What? And what else?"

Calvin grunts. Then he says, "Tell them I can see my left leg. Because it's right here by my face . . ."

"Yeah?" I think that does not sound good.

"Yeah. But I can't feel it. At all. It's dead asleep. In a bad way. And I'm thirsty, Mason. My head is aching. I'm scared."

"You hold on, Calvin!" I cry it out loud. "Hold on!" Then I run.

chapter 51

EMERGENCY

What happens is this: I yell. All through the crumble-down. "HELP! HELP ME! Uncle Drum! Grandma! HELP! I found him! I have Calvin!"

What I really have is Calvin's shoe. The tan-sandy. I tuck it into the waist of my pants. Then I crash through Grandma's kitchen to the sink. I fill a cup with water. Everyone comes. Uncle Drum first. Pulling on his blue jeans. Grandma and Shayleen follow straight after. We go stepping over the broken porch. Then all of us running. Water cup spilling. They follow me out back.

The four of us kneel in the brambles beside the hole. Flashlight shining down. We look and see Calvin's one foot. The dead-asleep foot. Shoe still on it. And just below, down in the hole, his white head. Wet. And muddy. Grandma reaches in. Touches Calvin's hair. She whispers, "Poor boy. We are here. Help is coming."

Uncle Drum says, "Damn! Oh! Damn! My god! Holy hell." Then he swears a bigger swear. He gets to his feet. He taps on his phone.

Shayleen says, "It'll be all right, Calvin. Little buddy."

I say, "He needs a drink!" They make room for me. I lower the cup down. Reach past Calvin's foot to find his face. Find his lips. He cannot take the cup. Not sure he can move his arms. I tip the water into Calvin. Not too much at a time. He sighs for the sips. I know when to give the next and the next.

Everyone is asking how such a hole got here. How deep does it go? How did Calvin get in it? And why? And why didn't we know it was here before now?

I say, "We dug it. We made the hole!" But it seems like nobody hears. No one except Calvin.

He takes tiny breaths to speak. He whispers, "Yep. We did. It was awesome." He says, "Sorry, Mason. Sorry about the root cellar . . ."

I try to tell him the cellar is fine—fine! But all the talking is drowned out by sirens. I look up from the hole. Red lights and blue lights flash through the orchard trees.

The yard at the crumbledown fills up quick.

There is the Merrimack Pee Dee. Then the fire

department. Rescue truck. All the volunteers. And searchers who have walked the whole night through. Feet come thundering. Voices come shouting. Equipment jingles. The sounds gather in my chest.

Calvin is an emergency.

I wave them to the place. Arm circles. Big as I can make. I warn about the thorns. I bring them to the top of the light shaft. I tell about the door down below. I give up the root cellar. I show everyone where Calvin Chumsky is.

Mr. and Mrs. Chumsky come. Tired faces. Smiles and tears. They hold their own knuckles. I show them the way to Calvin. And they are so so glad. They rush to see him. No one can believe it. How a boy can fit in a hole this way. How he ended up with one foot near the top and his head just below.

Tell you what I know. Calvin Chumsky is as slim as a wire. Now he's bent like one too.

chapter 52

EXTRICATION

"**S**tep back! Step back!"

I'm crowded out. Sent away. A woman takes charge. She says, "Emergency personnel only. Clear this area. *Please get back!*"

There is a plan to make. Some parts go quick. Uncle Drum moves the tractor. The firemen take the root cellar door off the hinges. They tear brambles and vines. They drag it all clear. Now the root cellar stands with its mouth wide open. Don't you know it, Lieutenant Baird arrives. He plants himself. Stands guard. People have come. From up the hill and down the hill. Coats over pajamas. Feet in their boots. They keep hands stuffed into pockets.

The rescue workers move inside. Then outside. So

many people in and out the small root cellar. They check top and bottom. Flashlights shining. They talk to each other. To Calvin. Then they measure things with their eyes.

I run alongside. Close as I can get. I call out, "It is five feet deep! Or might be six. It's a light shaft! Made from a Sonotube and—"

Lieutenant Baird turns his back to me. Arms wide. He pushes his elbows backward. He flaps his hand. He says, "Stay out of the way, Mason. Way out! *Extrication* is very tricky. Let them assess the situation. Let them work." Then he swings that arm back at me again.

I want to be everyplace. I want to be inside the cellar. And up at the top of the tube. I want to see Calvin.

But they have to set up tall lamps. They have to stretch the yellow tape. Equipment and rescuers are like a fence around Calvin.

I get an idea. I go inside and upstairs. I put my head out the window of the bedroom where I sleep. I hold the one tan-sandy shoe tight until I can give it back to Calvin. I look straight down. I can see the hole. And Calvin. Barely. But I know this: If he looks up—if he *can* look up—he will see me. Up here. In this window. He will know. I'm at the vantage point. I am with him. Much as I can be.

A digger comes. Slow roll off a flatbed. Vibrations jiggle the crumbledown. Rattle the window frames. The excavator bites through the brambles. Into the earth.

I smell the dirt. I smell the rain that came down in the night. They cut close to the shaft. So close to Calvin. Puts my heart in my throat.

But then a fireman comes running out from the mouth of the root cellar. Arms in the air. He warns the woman in charge. Something is not right. So she hollers, "Halt! Halt!" The digger lurches. Stops.

I put my head and shoulders out the window to see better. Tell you what. The crowd is some bigger now. I watch the digger crawl back. Away.

The woman goes to Calvin. Talks to him. I can't hear what. But I see her stretch her arms deep into the hole. I wonder, will she try to pull him out? Could I have done that?

But she doesn't try. She stands up. She says, "Where is the homeowner? I need dish soap. The whole bottle. Two if you have them."

And the bottles come quick. From Grandma's kitchen.

Then the woman says something about using *gravity*.

And I try to remember what I know about that. I think she means the weight of Calvin. The dropping down of him. Must be.

She pipes up. Tells the others, "We're going to keep him going in the same direction he was going. From the top down." She shows it with her hands. She says, "Are we ready below? The soap will *lubricate*. He will start to slide."

She says it like a promise.

Then there she goes. On her knees in the brambles. She reaches low with the dish-soap bottle. Arm deep in the hole.

Hard to see now. But she goes all around. Like making clock numbers. Smell of dish soap rises from the hole. Must be she is soaping the shaft. Must be she is squeezing soap all around all the sides of Calvin. All around inside that shaft.

She works with her arms way down in the hole. One, then the other. She says it. "Progress!" Calvin is dropping down. I hear her tell him, "Calvin, relax. Let yourself fall. There are many hands below to catch you."

And we wait and wait. Slow go that is. Sliding a boy down a tight skinny tube.

And then it is done! Out comes Calvin. Into the morning. There is cheering and clapping. It is for Calvin. For the rescuers. For an emergency that is over with.

I wave with both arms from the upstairs window. I holler Calvin's name. I see him seeing me—pretty sure. He holds up one pale thumb on one kitten-paw hand.

Calvin Chumsky is out of the hole!

chapter 53

TROUBLE FOR BREAKFAST

It's not much past sunup when the last rescue truck leaves. First one out took Calvin to the hospital. I came outside to watch them go. Now I stand in the quiet. Funny thing. I am awake to see a Wednesday night turn into a Thursday morning. Seems not real in the daylight now. All that has happened. I try not to worry. I try to believe that Calvin will be all right. They said so. They all said it. And he gave that thumbs-up. Pretty sure.

When I try to go back inside the crumbledown I see again what is left of our porch. Boards pulled up. I take the high step up into the house. I wonder how long that's going to stay like that. How long before we get new planks.

Inside Grandma has breakfast going. Scrambled eggs. Home fries. Uncle Drum is there. Turns out Lieutenant Baird stayed on. He is drinking coffee in the kitchen. But he's quiet. More than usual.

I don't ask it. I tell it. "Calvin peed on me. He couldn't help it. I need a shower. Right now."

Nobody disagrees with me. But Grandma passes me a basket full of clean, dry T-shirts before I head on up.

I let the warm water pour over me. I shampoo my head two times over. Just glad, is what I am. Glad and tired.

I come down. Clean. Sorry to see that the lieutenant is still here. Still drinking coffee. Might be that is all he wants. He has had a long night. Maybe that is why he is quiet.

I get a plate of breakfast in front of me. Smell the comfort of it. Then don't you know it, the lieutenant has got a question. He wants to know why I did not tell about Calvin and me and the root cellar.

I say, "It was a deal we made. Two friends. Because we didn't want those other kids to know." I put my fork in my eggs. Poke them.

He wants more. He says, "Which kids?"

I say, "Just the ones we have trouble with. The ones I told you about before."

He says, "Matt Drinker?"

I nod.

He says, "What kind of trouble?"

I say, "Apple fights and chases, is all. And some stuff about his dog."

He says, "So you and Calvin had a hideout? A place of your own?"

I say, "Yes."

Seems like the lieutenant understands. So I make the smallest smile at him. But he does not smile back.

He says, "This is a whole lot like what you told me about Benny Kilmartin, Mason. You realize this." The way he says it is not like a question. He says, "And so when Calvin went missing, you never thought to take me there? You never thought to tell the adults? You didn't think we'd want to know that there was a hole a boy could fit into?" The lieutenant leans close. I see the ugly green. Comes in from the sides of my eyes. A circle cloud. He says, "Why, Mason? Why is that?"

I hunch up. Wipe my sweat on my shoulder. Try to think of all the questions he just asked. I blink down hard on that fog of green. I say, "We didn't take my map. And I didn't know Calvin's map. So I didn't know he was there. And I just never—"

"Never what?"

"I never thought of fitting a boy in that hole. Because, like, why would I? That shaft, it was for light, is all."

The lieutenant scrunches his face at me. There is always something more he wants to know. I think about

Ms. Blinny. Just quick. How she said don't ever make up a thing to say just to make the lieutenant happy. Tell the simple truth. That's what she said.

The lieutenant says, "But why didn't you at least tell us that you had been playing in that old cellar?"

I say, "Well . . . I guess because . . ." I don't finish. He won't like what I say. Never does.

He says, "Why not, Mason? I want to understand this."

I say, "Because nobody asked!" Then I say it again. Louder. "Nobody asked!" Tell you what. The green is gone. Just gone.

I hear a voice. "Hey! Hey!"

Makes my head snap round. It's Uncle Drum. I wonder, is he yelling at me? For being so loud. But then he says, "That's enough now. Don't you think so, Lieutenant? Mason says nobody asked. He's right. We didn't ask." He looks at Grandma. She shakes her head. Sort of sad. Makes me sad too. Uncle Drum squares up to the lieutenant. He says, "Mason is nothing if not honest. You should believe him."

Tell you what. Feels good to hear that. Gives me some guts. I speak up. I say, "Lieutenant, I *did* check the cellar. On my own. I did. But I didn't think of the shaft part. Not until this morning. I don't know why."

Uncle Drum clears his throat. He says, "I checked that cellar too."

Now I am surprised. And the lieutenant is surprised.

Uncle Drum says, "I knew the boys had been down there some. Didn't know how much." He gives me a tiny nod. But he keeps talking to the lieutenant. He says, "So you bet I checked. I was sure it was empty. I admit it, I didn't know about the hole." Uncle Drum dips his chin. He says, "Probably should have."

The lieutenant says, "That seems pretty *negligent* to me, Drum." He points a finger at him.

Uncle Drum says, "Say what you will. But a person just cannot know what he doesn't know. And you can't always see that a bad thing is going to happen before it happens. If you could, no bad would ever come. Am I right? Don't you see that in your work, Lieutenant? Don't you see that plenty?"

Tell you what. I have got wide eyes on my uncle Drum. I cannot think when he has ever said so much all at once. I cannot think when something made so much sense.

Then the phone rings. Jolts us all. Me, up out of my chair. My fork flips off my plate. Shayleen pokes her head out like a cuckoo bird. We know this has to be the Chumsky parents. And it is. All heads turn toward Grandma while she takes the call.

Turns out Calvin is doing great. Great for a boy who got halfway folded up in a hole. Grandma listens, nods her head. Smiles. Her minnow eyes shine. Hand on her heart. She tells us, "No broken bones. But he sustained a concussion."

I say, "What is that? What does that mean?"

Uncle Drum says, "Hard knock on the head, Mason."

I say, "Oh, right. That headache he had. And he kept sleeping."

Grandma says, "There is some nerve damage in the leg and that will need time to heal. It will be months before he is one hundred percent. But they said his spirits are good."

I smile about that. Because it is a thing you could always say about Calvin.

Grandma says, "He is on the road to recovery. Could be he will come home as soon as tomorrow."

Then the lieutenant bursts right there in the kitchen. He says, "Phew! Lucky! We are so lucky." He breathes the good luck in and out.

I smile to see him that way. He smiles too. Everyone does. I think how same-side we are. He sets his empty mug on the kitchen counter. Grandma picks it right up. Soaps it with her sponge.

The lieutenant says, "Still, I will be asking."

I look at him and wonder, asking what?

He says, "I'm going to find out how the boy got into that hole. He'll be able to tell us."

Uncle Drum says, "Did you ever talk to those kids

from down the hill? Ask them what they saw?" He jabs a thumb toward the Drinker house.

The lieutenant says, "You know, we did. And they said just what Mason said." And now the lieutenant stops. He is giving me a sleepy kind of stare. All is quiet in the kitchen. A second. Or two. He snaps awake and says, "They said it was like Calvin disappeared. And I guess he did. Right into that hole. So he might have trouble remembering, what with the head injury. But I'm going to ask him how that happened. And I hope he can tell me."

I think it to myself: Good. I want to know that too.

chapter 54

CAVING IN

It is between bells when I get to the school. Halls are quiet. I head for the SWOOF. Ms. Blinny brings me right inside. Makes me think she has been waiting for me. She calls down to the office. She tells them she is keeping Mason Buttle for the rest of the day. It won't be all that long. I am super late. Tell you why. So much going on at the crumbledown this morning.

Ms. Blinny leans toward me. She says, "Oh, Mason. I heard what happened to you last night."

I say, "You mean what happened to Calvin? I am not the one that got stuck in the hole."

She says, "Yes, but how hard for *you* too. I'm sure it was a terrible night."

And she is right about that.

She says, "But you have heard, right? Calvin is going to be all right."

I nod when she says it. But this is when I find out how choked I am. I can't really speak to her.

Might be Ms. Blinny knows the feeling. She offers me the Dragon. She logs me in. I tuck the tissues under the earphones. I make two potato fists. Settle my forehead on them. Then I can talk.

I tell this to the Dragon:

Oh. Boy. I am glad to be in the SWOOF. For this whole day. What is left of it. Because I know there is a story. And it is rolling through this school like a stink bomb. Everyone probably knows. How I am the stupid kid who dug a dangerous hole. And Calvin fell in it. Tell you what. I have to plug my ears. I am too tired for it. The right parts and the wrong parts. The way it goes when people are talking and telling. Anyway. So umm I am tired because we searched. In the night. And I walked with the lieutenant. Baird. So umm we did find Calvin. Finally. That is the best thing. Still can't believe he was in the light shaft. That one we built in the root cellar. I can give that all up now. Because it is gone. Whole thing is.

See umm the town of Merrimack well they sent the building inspector over. This morning. Early. Before I came to school. Late. And it was not good news what they said to Uncle Drum. I mean. It's okay because umm I know you cannot really get all good news in one day. And we needed good news about Calvin most of all.

But the inspector well he said sorry. He said the root cellar was a condemnable hazard is what. Big danger. The inside ceiling was near to collapse. They said we could have lost that boy in there. Calvin. So. Then. The town, they sent the machine. Pretty big one. Digger on one end. Payloader on the other. Uncle Drum and Grandma let me stay home for it. So I was there to see when they set that big claw down on the roof of the root cellar. Sure did take a bite there. Like a dinosaur eats a meal. Ate the dirt first. Then it got down to where there was popping and cracking. Breaking. Tell you what. Less than one hour and they had dug away the whole top. They pushed it all into the cellar. Brambles. Broken boards. And our Sonotube. It is all piled right on top of where Calvin and I hung out. The man from the town said the old foundation umm the stone part could stay. So we have two walls standing up out of the ground now. Looks weird. Like they need something to go across the top of them. And they told Uncle Drum we better do that. Get some new boards. Cap it. For safety. Anyway the inspector said those walls are remarkable. And solid. Because things were built to last back in the time when the Buttle farm was new.

Well. So. It was hard to see it come down. And I guess I will have to tell Calvin our Caves of Lascaux got all crushed. Oh but umm one thing is still there. On one of those good old stony walls. The aurochs. Looks like he is standing in old boards and dirt now. Can't see his feet. It's too bad. But he is in the open now. Kind of like he is looking at the orchard. Feels best to think of it that way.

I stop talking. I sit. Keep my head down on my fists. I'm still as a rock. Someone else will want to get on this Dragon. Soon, I bet. But I don't move. Not yet. I think, maybe I should tell the Dragon more.

There is another thing that keeps coming. The bad-luck part. Like something dark that follows me. I worry. Seemed better for a while. But umm. I think it might. I think it is still there. What if we didn't find Calvin? I can't help it. I think how we lost things. Bing. Bang. Boom. Scares me. I know I made a big mistake. I didn't give up the root cellar. Should have. Like the lieutenant said. A person should know. I feel stupid. I feel dangerous. Makes me scared to be me. The way I am. Because what can you do about that. Nothing.

I feel a hand on my back. Did I stop talking? How long? I think, uh-oh, *Annalissetta Yang*! I pop my head up. Pull off that headset.

I'm wrong. It is Ms. Blinny. She whispers, "Sorry. I startled you." Then she pulls a tissue off the side of my head. She points to the screen. She says, "May I read?"

She is so kind the way she says it.

I say, "Sure." Already can't remember what I was writing. Then I know. I have been asleep at the Dragon. Just awhile. Then I think I should not say yes about her reading. But it is too late.

Ms. Blinny reads fast. She is looking at me. It's that way that I know she is seeing more than just my eyeballs. She sees *in*. She says, "Aw, Mason. I'm so sorry."

My jaw gets shivery. I try to stop it. Makes it worse.

Ms. Blinny says, "You know what happened? You learned something really important. That's your job as a kid. This crazy, awful experience is probably preparing you for a really great decision somewhere down the line. Something no one can even guess about yet." She smiles. She says, "How cool is that?"

I try to keep my jaw still. But it wants to shake. And it aches.

Ms. Blinny reaches into the basket on her desk. The flat glitter rocks with words on them. She holds one in her hand. She says, "Please. Don't be afraid. Live your big life, Mason! You are not bad luck. You're not stupid, or dangerous, or any of those things." She hands me the rock. She says, "This is you. *Loyal*. You are a loyal friend."

chapter 55

AUROCHS IN
THE ORCHARD

I sit by myself on the bus ride home. I hear the stink bomb of a story. Comes right up the aisle. The backseaters are talking about what happened to Calvin Chumsky. There is some lying going on.

I hear this: Calvin was upside-down in the hole. Blood rushed into his head and came out of his eyes. He was eaten by ants. He broke all his bones. He will never walk again.

I turn around. Look at the backseaters. I say, "No. He's recovering, Calvin is. We got a call at my house. He will be okay."

Lance says, "Buttle, who asked you?"

Matt says, "Yeah! Who did? And nice try, siccing the

cops on us. When the whole thing was your fault! Ha-ha-ha! The *hole* thing!"

I say, "Been wondering something . . . What did you see? Like, when you said you lost the pygmy. Yesterday. Part of that chase."

Tell you what, they look like they are thinking it over. Not trying to make up an answer. But like they aren't sure what the answer is. And Corey McSpirit is listening from the next seat over. I can see him looking on. Side eyes.

Matt answers me. Kind of serious. He says, "We already told the cops. We came around the house and he . . . I don't know." He looks at Lance. Then he says, "It was like the kid vanished."

Lance says, "What are you, Buttle? The big interrogator, here? If you or anyone thinks we stuffed that kid in the hole, you're wrong. We didn't even know it was there. And hey, Butt-hole, why do you have glitter on your sweaty mitts? Did you make arts and *craps* in the SWOOF today?"

I don't answer. I turn back. Sit straight in my seat. I know who I am. I am the best friend of Calvin Chumsky.

And the glitter is because I am *loyal*.

When we get to the cluster stop nothing happens. They do not chase me. They do not throw anything. I walk up to the crumbledown. Uncle Drum has put a sheet of plywood over those joists. Just loose. I step on it. It thumps and rattles.

I clomp along it and go inside. I sit at the kitchen counter. I ask Grandma has she heard any more news on Calvin. She says it's going well. The Chumsky parents still hope he can come home tomorrow. She will make them chicken dinner. Grandma hits the button on the blender. Makes one banana shake. She hands it to me. She says, "Maybe what you really need is a good nap." She might be right.

But I got some funniness about me. Tired. But moving all around. I don't know where to be or what to do. There is no root cellar. No Calvin. Moonie Drinker has not showed up. Wish he would. But wish he wouldn't. That could mean trouble for him.

I walk into the orchard. Not far. I turn and look back through the rows of trees. I see the back of the crumble-down. Sure is dug up and different back there. I see the root cellar. What is left of it. That heap. Uncle Drum has to decide about trucking that mess to the transfer station. Or maybe getting a dumpster.

I can see the two good walls and the aurochs from where I am. It's a strange thing my eyes do. And my brain. I know he is just charcoal and oil crayons on the old stony wall. And now a few scrapes from the digger. And his ankles are stuck under a mess of brambles and boards. But when I look through the apple branches—just the right way—it can look like he is *in* the orchard. Standing still.

I go up to our shed. Grab for the steel-toothed rake. I use that to free the aurochs. Just pull some of the mess from our *condemnable hazard* away from his feet. Then I smell maple and bacon.

Uncle Drum looks at the rake in my hands. He says, "We'll get that mess cleaned up, Mason. I'll figure it out. But probably better if you don't go climbing and picking around in there. Last thing you want is an old rusty nail in your foot."

I nod. I lean my chin on the rake. I say, "But can we really?" And I look at the aurochs instead of Uncle Drum. I say, "Can we get it cleaned up? And do like the town said. Put a new cap on it? I'll help."

Uncle Drum says, "We will do something. I promise."

chapter 56

NEW DIALOGUE

We sit down to dinner and nobody's talking much. But it's a better kind of quiet than we sometimes have. Like a golden kind of quiet because we know that Calvin is okay.

But then Shayleen hears the gravel popping out front of the crumbledown. She makes a dash for the window. Wants to see if it is the UPS truck. But I am thinking that he doesn't come this late.

Shayleen groans. Nose against the glass. She says, "Ugh! It's him again. Why doesn't he just pitch a tent in the yard? He's here morning, noon, and night anyway!"

I say, "Who?"

Shayleen says, "Lieutenant Baird."

Well, there goes anything that was good about supper. Got food turning cruddy in my gut before I get to eat much of it.

Grandma says, "Well, Shayleen. He had good reason to be here last night *and* this morning. There was a missing boy."

She is right. But I wonder what the lieutenant wants tonight. If it's not about Calvin and the root cellar, it will be about Benny. And I am thinking how I don't have anything new in that notebook for him.

Before he gets to the door I say, "Let's make sure he sees that the root cellar is gone. Make him happy."

Uncle Drum nods about that. But then he lets the lieutenant in. Doesn't mention it.

The lieutenant says he is sorry to arrive during our supper. Then he says he has been thinking of me all day. I believe him. He even looks like he is thinking now. Grandma and Uncle Drum and Shayleen all stay at the table while he talks. He doesn't ask for the notebook.

He says, "Mason, so much has happened in the last twenty-four hours. And after spending that time with you, I got an idea. I thought maybe we could start a new dialogue."

I think this: I am ready to talk about something new. Maybe there could be no interrupting.

I say, "Fine with me."

He says, "Did you ever go to the tree house alone?"

This does not sound like new dialogue. I scratch my head. Wipe sweat. I say, "Yes. Did that plenty. Because, you know, it's in the Buttle orchard. So. Closer to my house. And there was other stuff going on. Like, Benny had a tutor. One day a week. I can't remember which day. Not anymore. And then there were some days he had . . . I don't know what. Other stuff to do."

I finish. I think it is pretty good how long the lieutenant let me talk. He nodded, is all.

He says, "And you know how Benny fell down from that ladder. Right?"

I say, "Well, you told me. Weak rung."

He says, "I'm going to tell you something more. More of this puzzle. Something that I know, and it might surprise you that I know it."

I am already having trouble. Not sure what he means. Why would I be surprised?

He says, "You tell me if this sounds familiar. Tell me if it sounds like something you remember."

So now I listen. Not just with my ears. I listen with everything I am. With all the blood that runs inside of me.

He says, "Benny fell because somebody *tampered* with that top rung."

I say, "Tampered? I don't know . . . I tried to build that ladder right."

He says, "No, no. It's not how you built the ladder, Mason. It was sound. A good ladder. *Until* someone cut partway through the back of that rung."

I say, "Wait. Cut? You think somebody *sawed* on it?"

He points a finger at me—like to say that I am right about that. He says, "And I don't just think it. I know it. We can *see* that it was cut, Mason. And that's what we need to know more about. Somebody could do something like that just thinking it was a joke. A prank. Something silly."

I say, "Wait. Lieutenant." Now my mouth can hardly make the words. I say, "You think somebody . . . cut that on purpose? So it would break? With someone standing on it?"

He nods a slow nod. He says, "The cut looks like it was made with a handsaw."

I say, "*Handsaw.* Like mine? The one that has been missing?" The lieutenant stares a stare that says yes.

The silence puts a pain in my ear. Comes on so sudden. My breath is going all wrong. Dirt green is floating in. I say, "I remember . . . you asked me where my saw was. And if I threw it away somewhere in the orchard."

He still stares. Yes.

And then I think this: Threw it to hide it? So you wouldn't find it?

The lieutenant says, "Mason . . . I know how it is. Once

something goes so terribly wrong, fear can make a person do things tha—"

"You think it was *me* who did that." I gulp. *"Oh my god!"* There is so much green I cannot see the lieutenant. I say, "You think *I* sawed that rung. You think *I* did the thing that killed Benny Kilmartin."

chapter 57

THE BIG WRONG PIECE

Tell you what. When something is said, it is said for good.

It doesn't matter that now the lieutenant is saying that the handsaw is just something he thinks about a lot. And that he would like to know where that is.

I know what he thinks. I'm sick about it. I'm sick that my grandma heard. My uncle Drum. Shayleen.

I watch the lieutenant go out our door. I see ugly green puffs happening all on top of each other. I blink my eyes. I hear his shoes on the sheet of plywood out there. He's leaving. But he's staying inside of me. Because I know what he thinks. All the blood in me knows it and my heart knows it. With all of these dull thuds.

Uncle Drum and Grandma are talking. They try to comfort. They say there are still plenty of pieces to the puzzle. Shayleen's voice is there too. But I can't listen. I get up. Rush outside. I call to the lieutenant. It is dark but I see him beside his car.

I say, "Lieutenant! I need to tell you something."

I try to look at him. But I got this mess of sick green blobs. I try to speak but my voice croaks. It is hard knowing what he believes about me.

I say, "There have been a lot of times I have talked to you. And listened to you. And you say something and I say, yeah. To agree. Because it seems rude to say that you are not right. But you're not. You have things wrong. About me. There is a big *wrong* piece in your puzzle."

I see him nod. He says, "I would like for that to be true. The trouble is, Mason, I have to draw all conclusions on my own. You were the last one to see your friend alive."

There that is again. Makes me sound special. But it is not.

He says, "But you and I have a problem. I feel like you don't give me much to go on. You have the notebook. And you don't even have to write it by hand anymore. I told you the typing is fine with me. Fine."

I know the lieutenant is right about that. Takes me down to nothing but a whisper. I say, "I'm sorry! I am too *now and then* about it. I am that way about a lot of things."

He says, "And see, it's more important than that,

Mason. Finding out what happened to Benny should matter most of all."

The lieutenant tells me to think that over. When he drives away I wait there.

I start to think about all the sad-to-see-you faces in Merrimack. I *see* them. Andy and Franklin. And the clerk at Bishell's Hardware. Irene in her hairnet and Stewart at the grill. Margie up at Calvin's house. *All of them.*

I think this: It is not just the lieutenant who believes all this bad about me. I see dark on dark out here in the night. I blink. Then taste a splash of salt.

I put my hand in my pocket. Close sweaty fingers on the *loyal* rock. Smooth and round. I pull it out. Draw my arm back. I wing that rock across Swaggertown Road. I hear it hit pavement somewhere not far up on Jonagold Path.

I go back inside. Walk past my supper. On through to the stairs. I cannot look at Uncle Drum or Grandma or Shayleen. Not even when they call my name.

I go upstairs to the bed where I sleep. I roll up small. Small as a kid my size can be. And I close my eyes. Dig my fists into the sockets. And I sweat and sweat. And my heart pounds. Sicker and sicker. Because I get it now. All the sad-to-see-you faces are not just about me being Benny's friend and losing him. There are people who think I did something awful. They have been thinking it through two apple seasons. All this time I have been too stupid to know that.

chapter 58

THE BEST BOY

I am up and at the kitchen counter before daylight. I'm
awake because of what the lieutenant said. I have the
notebook open. Right in front of me. Those couple of
Dragon writing pages sticking out of it. I don't put on the
light. No point. It's not like I can write in it. I keep sticking the point of that orange pencil into the fold. Watch it
stand. Then watch it fall.

I think about what the lieutenant said. That I haven't
given him much. Then I try to remember what more I
have said into the Dragon. I know some is about Benny.
And the tree house. I wonder if something there could be
a piece that he needs. A piece to make him believe in me.
Trouble is, I have already told all of it to him. Way back.

Grandma comes in. She whispers, "Oh . . . Mason, honey." She says it because I am here, is all. And it is way early. She puts on the light. Tunes her National Public Radio. Just low. She starts the coffee. Then she leans on the counter.

She says, "You okay, Mason?"

I shake my head no. I say, "I couldn't sleep. Just can't believe . . . well . . . about the lieutenant. And all that."

She says, "I know." Her voice is soft.

I say, "He really thinks it. Thinks I did something to hurt Benny. And he thinks I lied about it too."

Grandma sighs. She says, "He seems to have an idea that he can't let go of."

I say, "Yes! That's it! It's killing me, Grandma. Like a hole gone through. Like losing Benny again. Sort of."

She says, "We have to try to understand how hard his job is. He has to piece together a story. But he also has to prove it."

I say, "I want him to have the true story. For everyone. And . . . because, Grandma, I think this is bad. What if . . . well . . . couldn't I be in a lot of trouble?"

Then I see it. Her eyes fill up. Tears drowning the minnows.

I say, "Grandma, did you ever think it? This whole time? That I did it? Did you think I hurt Benny?"

She flicks the water out of her eyes. She says, "Not for a minute. And neither did your uncle Drum. But what's even more important is that we know you don't lie, Mason. That's why we decided it'd be okay for you to talk to the lieutenant. We could have refused. But we know you are a good boy. The best boy."

She reaches. Takes my earlobe in her finger and thumb. I forgot she used to do this. When I was small. She rubs it—little squishes, like I am dough. She looks me over and I feel like I am small. So small. Like my own mom—gone so long—will walk into the room behind me. And why that? Why? When I cannot even remember her so well. Why do I feel her now? I don't ask it out loud. I don't think anyone could answer.

Grandma gets breakfast started. I lay my head down on my arms. Close down on my eyes. Kind of like I am going to tell something to the Dragon. But I know I'm not at school. I am home. I'm glad for it. The kitchen is warm. Coffee smell in the air. I still feel small and tired. So tired.

I think this: Grandma knows I wouldn't saw up a rung. She knows I wouldn't lie. She said I am the best boy . . . best boy . . .

Then there is Shayleen. Standing beside me. She says, "Ew! Your head is touching the counter. Mason. Ew! Sit up!"

I do that. I look around the kitchen. See Grandma at the far end. She is pulling laundry out of the dryer now.

National Public Radio is up a little louder. Sun is coming in.

Shayleen says, "Here. I got you something." She slaps down a package. Bandanas. Folded stack. Must be six. All colors. She says, "These are one hundred percent cotton. I got them during Made in the USA week on the shopping channel. You need to carry one of these all the time. Always, always. Actually, you might need two because you sweat like a . . ."

She thinks that over.

She says, "You sweat *excessively*. These will help."

I say, "Thank you?" Comes out of me like a question because I am confused. She is sort of yelling at me. But being nice. Because she did buy me something. But then I wonder who paid for the bandanas anyway?

Shayleen says, "And Mason, I know you are upset. You have good reason. But you need to get a grip. Because that lieutenant is way off when it comes to you. Okay? You hear me?"

I nod. Because I sure hear her. She is right in my ear.

She says, "Now, I'm also going to get permission from Drum and order you some new pants. You're thinning out and shooting up. And you're going to need a razor because your chin is fuzzy."

I gulp. Slap my hand over my chin. I do not want Shayleen talking about chin hairs.

She says, "Now swab that sweat."

So then I sit here with my new bandanas. I pull on my chin to check for hairs. While I do that I wonder how it was that Shayleen got all flipped around to where she is for me instead of against me.

I take a bandana. The pink one. Open up the wide square. I think this: Pink is the color of good. So maybe the bandana can bring some to me.

chapter 59

THE TRUTH FROM
THE DRAGON

The bus takes the loop through town. It is quiet. Not
so many kids riding. That is partly because this is
the Friday running right into Columbus Day weekend.
Some families cut out early. Not the Drinkers. They will
leave this afternoon. Anyway, I have my seat to myself.
I sit up high. I'm keeping up with Merrimack. Watching for all my checkpoints. But tell you what else I do. I
think.

What I decide is this: I need to stop being *now and then*
about all the things I am *now and then* about. I need to do
things right. Better. In my head I make a checklist. Hope
I can remember it all. This morning, I need to get to the
Dragon. And I need Ms. Blinny's help.

In the SWOOF I find Annalissetta Yang. She is standing near to the Dragon. About to sit down. That is not a good start. Not for me.

I tell Ms. Blinny, "I need something. Real bad." I say, "I need to print from the Dragon again. I can't wait through the long weekend. Columbus."

I think she knows I need something for the lieutenant. She says, "Oh. Okay. I have two afternoon meetings. Hmm . . . let's see when we could do that?" She looks at the clock. She looks at a list on her desk. Then she looks at Annalissetta Yang.

Annalissetta smiles with her tiny teeth. She says, "You want my turn, Mason? Want the Dragon now?"

I say, "If you could give it to me. Please."

She says, "Sure. That's okay with me."

Ms. Blinny says, "Annalissetta, you are very kind."

Annalissetta says, "Not a problem!"

I tell her that I owe her a favor.

Annalissetta says, "I will hold you to it, Mason." She turns her Crocodile around. Away from the Dragon desk. She goes to the soft couch. She gets busy with a book.

I whisper. I tell Ms. Blinny what the lieutenant told me. How he thinks bad of me.

She is quiet about it. She says, "We're going to find what you need." She scrolls through all the things I have fed to the Dragon. There is a lot of writing here for a kid like me. Surprised to see it. I wipe my face with the pink bandana from Shayleen. I watch over Ms. Blinny's shoulder. Try to read. The letters blur. They fatten up. Go splotchy.

I tell Ms. Blinny, "I am looking for something that was about the last time I saw Benny. It is about me jumping down from the tree house."

She scrolls some more. She says, "Oh, here! Here!" Then she reads it. She does not skim. She is careful. She stops. Looks at me. She says, "One second." She reads it all again. She breathes out. She says, "Ohh . . ."

I wait for her. Then I say, "Does it make sense? Mostly?" I ask because I know the Dragon is tricky. I am not the best at using it.

She says, "Mason, I think this is very, very good." She says, "One thing is certain. Lieutenant Baird *needs* to see this. There is so much of your story here. More than I think you have ever been able to tell him." She is getting tears in her eyes. Not sure why. She says, "I wish I had—known that you see colors in this way." She points at the screen.

I say, "You mean that part about the pink cloud puffing out of Benny's mouth?"

She says, "Yes."

I say, "I don't tell about it. I figured out that nobody really gets that."

She says, "Yes! Because it is *uncommon* but it is *real*. Real for you! It is called *synesthesia*." She makes bright eyes like I should like that a whole lot, that *synesthesia*. She says, "I had a student in another school who told me all the even numbers are yellow and the odd ones are blue. Some people say they can smell a color. Or hear one."

I say, "Whoa!" I wait. But then I tell her, "With me it is the feeling. Inside of me. Like coming from in my heart. I see mud green for bad. Like for pressure. And not knowing the answers. It's pink for the good. Like for being happy."

She says, "Wow! Amazing!" She puts her hand on her heart.

I think on it some. Then I shake my head. I tell Ms. Blinny, "But can you delete it?" I point to the Dragon screen. "I don't want to bother with that part for the lieutenant. I don't want him to read about the pink cloud puffing out of Benny's mouth."

She sits tall in her chair. She says, "I will if you really want me to. But I would much rather you leave everything just like it is. This is clean and straightforward."

I say, "But the lieutenant thinks that's a bunch of baloney. I've told him all of it before. But he stops me at that part. He interrupts."

She says, "Well. I think if he reads it here, just like this, he might understand *all* the truths of your story." She says, "I say we print it."

I wonder. I worry. But Ms. Blinny is usually right. So we do that.

I get home on Friday afternoon. I put that print-out from the Dragon right into the notebook. With the orange pencil.

Then I run down to the Drinker house. It's the beginning of Columbus Day weekend. I have a job to do. A great one.

chapter 60

COLUMBUS DAY COMES

Mrs. Drinker is excited to go away for Columbus Day weekend. They are going to see Matt's dad. He is traveling again for his work. Staying somewhere in a nice hotel. Fancy room and a warm swimming pool. So they will join him.

She is talking a blue streak. She says, "There is dog food in the bin. Plenty, I think. But just in case, a delivery is on the way. I tracked it. They said late afternoon today. So should be here anytime now."

Matt Drinker is sighing. A lot of times over. He leans against the wall. Playing a game on his phone. Jacket on. Stuffed backpack at his feet. He doesn't look up. But a couple of times now he has said, "Mom. Are you kidding me? Let's go already!"

Mrs. Drinker keeps her eyes on me. She says, "So Mason, the new dog food gets stored in the garage until the indoor bin is empty. It's a huge bag but if you can please get it onto the shelves out there, that's the best place." She says, "Sometimes the rain blows in under the door—and it does look like it'll rain—and that can ruin the whole bag. So keep it high and dry."

I say it. "High and dry." The rhyme will help. I won't forget.

Matt stamps a foot. He says, "Let's just go. Mom! We're going to miss the flight."

Then Mrs. Drinker keeps thinking of one more thing to tell me. About the mail. About the thermostat. About the lights at night. About Moonie's water bowl. But I already know.

Matt groans about all of it. But he keeps tapping his thumbs on his phone. I hear the sounds. *Pow-pow-pow!*

I listen to Mrs. Drinker. Best I can. I am blink-eye tired. If that is even a thing. It's good that I already know how to take care of Moonie.

Now Mrs. Drinker wonders if she should write every-thing down for me. I tell her that won't help me much. Then she remembers. She says, "I'm sorry." She forgot I am not a reader.

Matt rolls his eyes. Pretty sure he mouths *stupid* into the air. Then he goes back to clicking around on his game. I think of that shirt he made me. The STOOPID one. How Ms. Blinny made it into a curious statement. It was early apple season then. Paula Reds and Macs. Here we are now. Late season.

Mrs. Drinker picks up her bag and her keys.

Matt says, "Finally!" He starts kicking his backpack toward the door.

Mrs. Drinker says, "Pick it up, Matt." Then she turns to me. "Mason, we cannot thank you enough. There is no one we'd rather leave our Moonie with."

I think this: It is going to feel good to be with him.

She stops. Leans down and hugs up the dog. She says, "Be a good boy for Mason, Moonie. Good boy!" He wags and leans into her. He kisses her good-bye.

And then there I am alone at the Drinkers' house. With the best dog in the world. I am welcome to eat from the Drinkers' fridge and pantry. I can play games here. I can be here as much as I want. I have to put Moonie in for the night and make sure I get back in the morning to let him into the yard. It's easy. I would never forget him. I am all in for this dog. Moonie is all in for me too. He is resting beside me. Chin on my foot.

Here's the thing. Calvin is home and I am aching to see him. The Chumsky parents said I am invited to visit and I can bring Moonie too.

But I have this job. I want to do it right. Been a day of gray skies. Could mean rain. So I decide to wait for that dog food delivery.

I take Moonie out. Throw a ball for him. I keep watch. Up and down the street for the truck. Tell you what. Funny feeling it is. Playing in Matt Drinker's yard with nobody else around.

Moonie barks when the UPS truck pulls into the drive. I say hello to Jerald. Same driver who drops off all Shayleen's shopping channel merchandise. Moonie puts two feet on the step of the truck. He is polite about it. Jerald hands him a biscuit. Then that dog wags while Jerald passes the bag down the steps of the truck to me. It sure is a big bag of dog chow. Jerald says, "Thirty pounds. Sure you can manage it?"

I can. I put it on my shoulder. Steady it with one hand. Wave good-bye with my other. I carry the bag right into the Drinkers' garage.

I see the shelves. There is some space kind of low. Some way up. I remember *high and dry*. So I balance that bag on my shoulder. Kick open the Drinkers' stepladder and climb up. I raise the bag, push it into place. Takes a couple of big shoves. Tell you what. It can be good to be tall. Then I wipe my hands. Pull up on my pants. All the time Moonie sits below. He is waiting for what we will do next. I come down the stepladder. Fold that up.

I tell Moonie, "Come on! Let's go!"

He springs off all four feet. We climb the hill. Through the orchard to the crumbledown. I stop in there. Dog follows me in the door. Shayleen pokes her head out of the room that used to be mine. Says, "Nah-uh, Mason. No dog. Not inside."

There you go. Shayleen is her old self again.

I hear Grandma call out. She says, "The dog is fine." Her words go well with the smell of a roast chicken dinner that is about pressing out the walls of the house.

I stay just long enough to grab one thing: a tan-sandy shoe. Then I'm back out the door with Moonie. I take him across Swaggertown. Fingers under his collar. Just gentle. Just careful. When it's safe I let him go. We head up Jonagold Path to be with Calvin.

chapter 61

VISIT WITH CALVIN

Inside the Chumsky house I am welcome. So is Moonie.
Margie is not here. The Chumsky parents are both
home from their jobs. Both meet me in the front hall by
the door. They say they want to be with Calvin. To make
a fuss. And cookies. And all of Calvin's favorite foods.
And to help him get well again too. There are no sad-to-
see-you faces. They hug me. Both of them do. *Me.* I think
about what Calvin said. Sometimes the Universe gives
you what you need. The Chumsky house feels that way
today.

I say, "Can I see him?"

They say, "Of course!" And the feeling, it is like a
birthday present.

They lead me in and there is Calvin. He is on their couch kind of laid back. Lots of pillows. And I don't much like seeing that there is a wheelchair too. But he looks like himself. Whole and skinny and with his white kitten hair standing up on his head. Like it should.

He calls, "Mason! Moonie!"

Glad to see us. He pats the cushion beside him and Moonie stands on hind feet. Wagging. He licks Calvin's ear. Gentle. Almost like he is being careful of him. Then that dog climbs up next to Calvin. Not bouncy. Just calm. He curls in beside him. Chin on Calvin's hip.

I hand Calvin his tan-sandy shoe. He grins. He says, "Ha! Nice rescue." He claps the shoe against his palm.

I say, "I am so glad you're okay. Well, mostly okay."

He says, "I'm so glad you saved me!"

I say, "You are a lot cleaner than the last time I saw you." It is a joke. True and funny. Makes Calvin laugh.

Then I tell him, "I'm sorry I was so dumb. I should have given up the root cellar sooner. Then you wouldn't have been stuck in there all night long. And your leg wouldn't have gone so dead asleep. Must have been awful being squeezed inside the tube like that."

Calvin says, "Well. That was the one advantage to banging my head so hard."

I say, "That concussion?"

He says, "Yeah. I was out cold—a lot of the time. Or, I think. When I did wake up, well, everything was weird inside that tube. Some of it seemed like I was still dreaming. The rest of the time I told myself not to panic. Mind over matter." Calvin sighs. He says, "I'm not interested in doing it again. Tell you that much."

I say, "Holy cow! No! Never."

He says, "By the way, you weren't stupid, Mason. We had a pact. And you didn't break it until you had to."

I whisper to Calvin. I say, "Still. I feel stupid."

He says, "Mason, *I* was stupid."

I say, "No way!"

He fiddles with the shoe. He says, "You might change your mind about that. See, I was foggy when they first pulled me out. But I've been remembering parts of what happened."

"Really? Was it them? Do you know? Did Matt and Lance shove you into that hole?" I stop. I think that is too many questions.

He shakes his head no. He says, "It was *me*, Mason. I jumped into that shaft."

I open up my eyes wide. I think this: Calvin disappeared.

Calvin says, "They were on my tail. And here is another stupid thing. I don't even think I was scared of them. I just wanted to win at the chase. Somehow. And I wanted to get to the root cellar but still keep it a secret. So I had this idea. Like a flash. I thought the shaft could be the fastest way down to the root cellar. Like the laundry chute at your house. Do you know what I mean?"

I say, "Uh . . . yeah . . . guess so. But tell you what. I think I am too big of a kid to think that up. Because I would never fit in there."

Calvin laughs. He says, "I had to ditch my backpack."

I say, "We found that! Behind the mousey chair!"

Calvin says, "I must have stashed it there. I don't remember. But it had to be right after that when I kicked the cap off the hole. I can kind of remember Shayleen's salad bowl sailing off to one side."

I say, "We never got that adhesive."

"Nope. So there it was. An open hole. I knew if I held myself tight and straight—like, arrow-narrow—I could jump and make it down the shaft. But . . ." He holds the tan-sandy shoe up and waggles it. He says, "My toe must have caught on the rim of the tube. Just that one foot. But all the rest of me was heading downward. So . . ."

I say, "Gravity."

Calvin says, "Exactly. Freak accident. All the EMTs and the doctor said it: You probably couldn't make it happen twice. Not if you tried. They aren't even sure how I knocked my head." Calvin shrugs. He says, "It doesn't really matter. Except that I'm curious."

Then I say, "You could have made it all the way down, Calvin. If your foot had not caught you would have."

He nods. He says, "I really could have. I'm sure of it."

I think about it. I say, "But then maybe I would have found you on the cellar floor. Like with two broken feet. From the landing."

Calvin says, "Maybe. Or I could have landed just fine and had the best story to tell." He stops to grin. Then he says, "Instead I get this bum leg." Calvin taps on his thigh.

I say, "Does it hurt a lot?"

He says, "Pretty miserable. The worst thing about a dead leg is when it wakes up again. The doctor told us nerves are slow to repair. So I have the wheelchair and a walker. I have to do physical therapy. I'm going to hate that. But they give me medicine. It helps."

I say, "I'll help you too. Anything you want. I could carry you! And Calvin. You know what? There is good glory. Because you *did* win. You ditched them, Matt and Lance. They think you disappeared."

He smiles. Tilts his head. He says, "Yeah. I guess I did. And victory always has a cost."

Then I ask him, "Hey, what did you dream? While you were sleeping in that hole?"

Calvin looks like he is trying to remember. He says, "Mostly, I dreamed about being squished. You know how some dreams blend in pieces of real life? And there was something about the belly of a dog. And I think it was Moonie."

Funny thing. Moonie hears his name. Lifts his head.

Calvin reaches out to pat him. He says, "I dreamed he sailed over the hole. Over my head. Maybe even over the whole entire root cellar hill."

I like the dream. I say, "Well, he is a mighty dog."

Calvin and I pat Moonie's back. His soft round head. And we are quiet for a minute.

But then I have something to tell Calvin. The thing I don't want to say. But I do. "You know it's gone now? I mean, the root cellar."

He says, "I knew it would be." He says, "Sorry, Mason."

I say, "It's okay. We'll find something else to do."

chapter 62

MOONIE HOUDINI

I get back to the crumbledown with Moonie and don't you know it, Grandma has made two chicken dinners. One for us. One to pack up for the Chumskys. She wants me to turn around and take that up there. Moonie sniffs the air. Likes the smell of chicken dinner.

I say, "Hmm. It's time for Moonie to eat too."

Grandma nods. She says, "Okay, do that first. But scoot, because we want to deliver this hot."

So I call Moonie. We run down to the Drinker house. I get him chasing an apple all the way. Gets us there fast.

At the house I fill his bowl from the bin. Set it down

and get out of the way. Tell you what, that dog eats fast. Always has. I get him out back in the fenced part of the yard. Mrs. Drinker says he will *relieve* himself. I know he will. He's usually quick about it. But tonight he takes his time.

I think of that hot chicken dinner for the Chumskys. Then I think, this dog does not need me to watch him *relieve* himself. Might be he'd like to do that on his own.

So I tell him, "I'll be right back, Moonie boy." I give him the *stay* hand. And run back up the hill. My shirt is wet. I can't be a gross-out dropping off a chicken dinner. So I run upstairs, pull off my shirt, and grab a fresh one. I pop my head through. Just happen to see out my window. Vantage point. Down into the Drinkers' yard. It's empty. Except for Moonie. Funny thing. He is trotting in a circle. Then he starts to gallop. He makes one wide run around the yard. He bounds onto the seat of their outdoor couch. Then he sails over the fence like it's nothing.

I say, "Holy cow!"

I watch that dog. He hits the ground running and he does not stop. He comes at a gallop straight up through the orchard. Smiling jaw. Pink tongue. I run downstairs. Open our door. There he is standing on the plywood. Waiting for me. Marching steps. Wagging tail. And the thin color of raspberry pink all around him. I hug him up. I make a guess: He has escaped like that about a hundred times before.

Now I can tell Matt and his mom how Moonie gets out. It is not me stealing him. He gets out on his own. Pretty much whenever he wants to.

Now I know.

chapter 63

CHICKEN DINNER

When we sit down to our own chicken dinner I ask it straight out. I say, "Can we please call the lieutenant." I say it right there. To everyone. Even Shayleen.

Uncle Drum says, "Why? You think he won't come by soon enough?"

Shayleen says, "He will. You know he will." Then she turns to me. She says, "Are you using those bandanas, Mason? Did you bring one to the table? Got a favorite color? Because I can get you some more. And remember the other items we talked about?" She flicks her fingers under her chin.

But I do not want to talk about bandanas. Or getting new pants. Or the fuzz on my chin.

I say, "I got that writing for him. Something I printed out at school. I want the lieutenant to read that. I don't want to wait. I know we have his number. He gave that to us way back, right?"

Grandma says, "We have it."

She does not say more. Then I think maybe I have put a cramp in our chicken dinner. So I tell Grandma how good it is. Juicy. Salty. Perfect. Makes her smile.

Well, it gets quiet. The way it is around our table. I eat my chicken. I think about all the questions I would like to be talking over. Like, can we get down to Bishell's Hardware and pick up some boards for the porch? Like, are we going to get a dumpster? Or can we haul that mess out of the old root cellar in the back of the truck? I look at Uncle Drum. Picking up a lump of mashed potato with a piece of chicken. He tucks that in his cheek. Looks up and stares off. I think all my questions are not the things Uncle Drum wants to talk about right now. I just have that feeling.

I say, "So hey. Do you all want to know about Calvin?"

Grandma says, "Oh yes!"

Shayleen says, "Yeah, yeah, yeah! Tell."

Uncle Drum turns to look at me.

I say, "He's got a leg nerve all waking up. Says it hurts like fire and nettles. But he is tough." Then I tell about the wheelchair. How I gave his shoe back. And how Calvin got into that hole in the first place. I say, "He wanted to win that chase. And he did. He really did." I say the part about the cost of victory.

Then I say, "You want to know something amazing about all those Chumskys up there?" I point my fork up toward Jonagold Path.

Shayleen says, "Mason! Watch it!"

I say, "Sorry." I set down the fork.

Grandma says, "Tell us. What about the Chumskys?"

I say, "After all the bad that happened, they want to come and see."

Shayleen huffs. She says, "See what?"

I say, "Oh. The root cellar. I mean, what's left of it. They don't think bad about us for it. You know what I mean?"

Uncle Drum says, "That's good of them."

Grandma says, "It's nice to know that someone chooses to think the best of you. When they could do just the opposite."

She makes me think of the lieutenant. Can't help it.

She sighs. "That whole incident, though, it was a bit of a wake-up call." She shakes her head. "We need to do better." I look over at Uncle Drum. I see him nodding a big slow nod. Grandma says, "We need to take a few steps."

After we clear, after Grandma is done in the kitchen, I ask again. I say, "Can we call him. The lieutenant?"

She reaches into a little basket. Place she keeps loose stuff together. She holds up a card. Number on it. She says, "Do you want to speak to him? Or shall I?"

I bump my thumb on my chest. I pick up the phone. She reads me the number.

I dial. And I do get him. He picks up.

He says, "Mason!" Like he is glad it's me.

Might be he feels like I do. I like the faraway of his voice. I like this phone between us. Still have to steady up to talk. But I do it.

I say, "Just so you know . . . I put a page into the notebook."

He says, "Did you now?"

What he tells me is this: He will come. But he is away from Merrimack. A few days of vacation this Columbus Day weekend.

He says, "I will see you, though, Mason. You bet. Be there Tuesday. After school." Then he says, "And Mason. Thanks so much for the call."

chapter 64

COLUMBUS DAY WEEKEND

All the rest of Columbus Day weekend I go from the Drinkers' house to the crumbledown to the Chumskys' house. I am pretty busy. Caring for Moonie. Doing double checks for laundry. Getting that all up off the bedroom floor and down the chute. I run the vac over the carpet in the living room. Tell you what. Makes paths where I suck up the dirt. We are too *now and then* about it, is why. Moonie tips his head. Listens to dirt bits going up the hose. And even Shayleen pops out to watch him. Smile on her face. And tell you what. That carpet looks not so bad when I am done.

We go up and see Calvin. He is practicing standing. Putting weight on the fire leg. Drawing circles with his foot. Point and flex. Moonie walks on elbows next to Calvin. He wags when I cheer.

It is all funnier and better with Moonie Drinker to join in. Helps me get my brain off what the lieutenant thinks about me. Off the sad-to-see-you faces. The troubles. And when all of that does come crashing at me, well, it doesn't seem to crash as hard.

Monday evening comes. Bittersweet, is what it is. I give Moonie his supper. Still a few scoops left in that bin. He gets all *relieved* outside. Comes right back in when I call him.

I lie down on the family room floor at the Drinkers' house. The dog comes to me. He bows down on his dog elbows by my side. Puts his head on my chest. He noses up and licks me. Takes care of my sweaty neck. Chin to earlobes. He puts out a warm wet breath. That goes right from his two nose holes straight into my ear. Tickles like crazy! Like being poured full of sunshine and soda bubbles. Makes it clear to my middle.

I think, what else is like this? This good? What in the whole wide world? Nothing!

I hug him up. Pat him over and over again. Stroke, stroke, stroke, Moonie Drinker. My hand fits his smooth head bone. I hold his ear in my fingers. Give it some squishes. Feels nice as a sock just come out of the dryer. I tuck my thumb on the underside and scratch. Moonie tilts his whole head. Goes just about upside down for more. Then he rests his chin. I feel him take swallows against my shoulder.

I say, "You're a good boy. Best boy."

I hate to leave him. But his family is coming home. My job is done.

I think this: I had great luck to crash my sled through the Drinkers' cellar window. Well, at first it was pretty bad. But it turned pretty good.

I tell Moonie good night before I go back home. I put on National Public Radio for him. Just low. Hope Moonie won't be lonesome in the empty Drinker house.

chapter 65

SMARTER

I have one of those mixed-up days at school. I mean I guess it goes okay. If you are looking at me from the outside. But what I know is that I miss Calvin. I miss Moonie. And I kind of miss the clean carpeting at the crumbledown all because I made it look better.

But I get a chance to tell Ms. Blinny about Calvin. His recovery. She is glad to hear that he's doing well. She notices my bandana. Light-blue one today. I tell her it is a gift from Shayleen. Sort of. Then she asks after Shayleen. I think it might be the first time I say it: "She is pretty okay."

Ms. Blinny says, "Anything else to tell me, Mason?"

I know it means she has an idea about what.

She leans forward. She says, "Did you get to share your

Dragon notes? With the lieutenant?" Makes a smile like she cannot wait to know.

I say, "Not yet. Turned out he wasn't around this weekend. But he's coming today. I am pins and needles about it. But I want to cooperate. I hope you will be right about him seeing all the truths."

End of the school day, I get on the bus. Soon as he sees me Matt Drinker calls out from the back. He says, "Nice work, Butt-head. My dog *smells*. Like *your* sweat. Like he is coated in it." I open up my eyes wide. Feel my face go red. I try to cover that with a swipe from the blue bandana.

He says, "My mom has to take him for a bath today. Because of you."

I land on a seat. Try to get small. I think this: Could that be true? I do touch Moonie a lot. And I am real sweaty. But I am not stinky. I make sure of that. I even asked Shayleen if I was. I put my armpit up for her, and tell you what. If I stank, she would tell me. But Matt has me worrying. I think this: What if Mrs. Drinker never asks me to dog-sit again? Then there I am seeing some of that muck-green fog.

On the loop through town I watch for the Merrimack Pee Dee. The cruiser is there. Number 003. Lieutenant Baird's car. So then I know. He is not at my house. Not yet.

Off the bus at the cluster stop I take a chance. Walk straight away for home. I don't get far. A lacrosse ball stings me—back of my thigh. Kind of takes that leg out. I stop. Breathe out. Turn around. Another ball comes sailing my way.

I reach. I catch. I do one turn on one foot. Try to absorb that sting. And oh, man. That smarts. I look back at Lance and Matt. And Corey McSpirit, standing off to the side. I hold the ball up. I show it. Last thing I am going to do is throw it back. Give them another shot.

I say, "You dropped this." Not quite true. More like somebody winged it. I set that ball down on the gravel. Right next to my big sweaty feet.

I say, "If you want it, it'll be right here."

I turn and head to the crumbledown. I don't run. I walk. And nothing happens. I think this: Holy cow, Mason Buttle. You are getting smarter.

Inside the crumbledown Grandma greets me. She has a message. From Mrs. Drinker. I am worried this will be about my sweat. On her dog. But Grandma says, "She needs your help moving a big bag of dog food. She said you would know."

I say, "Oh, right. Might be Moonie's bin is empty. Might be Mrs. Drinker needs me to reach that."

I think this: *too* high and dry.

I ask Grandma to hold off on making my banana shake. I say, "I'm going to run down there now. Get it off my mind. Because the lieutenant could be here. Any minute. And I can't be thinking about both those things. So Grandma, if he shows up, give him the notebook. I'll be right back."

chapter 66

MY GREAT REACH

I am standing alone in the Drinkers' garage. Looking up. Guess I did put that bag up pretty high. I open up that stepladder pretty much quick as I can. Gotta get this done.

Funny thing, me wanting to get back for a meeting with the lieutenant. First time for that. I got some hope about the writing piece from the Dragon. My true story about Benny Kilmartin.

I climb up. I reach high for the bag of dog food. Just have to slide it to me.

In comes Lance Pierson at the small side door. Matt and Corey behind him. They start looking through a bucket of lacrosse sticks and sports stuff. Lance spots me first. He says, "Oh great. Look. Buttle's butt crack! Just what we want to see."

I reach back. One hand. Tug up my pants. But I think this: I am busy here. Can't worry about what's behind me. I need to get this done. I grab the thick paper sides of the dog food bag. I grunt. Pull it toward me.

Matt pipes up. Sharp ring in his voice. He says, "Hey! What are you . . . what are doing up there?" I look down at him. He is all shifty feet. Funny thing, he looks scared for me to be on this ladder.

So I tell him, "I'm fine, I'm fine. I'm getting the dog food. I put it up too high. Made a mistake."

Lance says, "Buttle, you *are* a mistake." He snorts. Matt doesn't laugh. Neither does Corey McSpirit.

I turn back to the shelf. Reach fingers around the bag again and don't you know it, something bites me—and I mean with *teeth*. "Yow!" I pull my hand back. I take a look at my fingers. Three of them have bloody scrapes. In rows. They all sting like heck. More blood comes up. I wipe that on my shirt.

Lance says, "Ugh! Disgusting! Now I'm gonna barf." He coughs.

But Matt shouts over him. He says, "G-get down, Buttle! Just get down!" He keeps shouting that at me. Waving his arms at me.

I can't think what's gotten into him. And now I see fake-puking Lance. He is giving Matt a weird look. Like he wonders the same thing. And Corey too. Whatever. I am going to get this bag down for Mrs. Drinker. And Moonie. I'm careful not to stick my fingers in the same spot. I grip the end of the bag and tug it. Once. Twice.

Matt says, "Leave it! Just leave it, Buttle!"

I don't know what he's thinking. I'm the tallest. Not like he can reach. And the bag is heavy. And besides, *I* put it here. It should be me who brings it down.

I get it to the edge of that shelf and heft it to my shoulder. Same second, something slides off the shelf. Drops down in front of me. Skims me. Happens quick. Something long and flat is all I see. It hits the floor. I try to look. But all of a sudden I got kibble spilling down the front of me. Pinging. Bouncing. Onto the floor of the Drinkers' garage. Then I know it. I have a rip in this bag. I go grabbing at it. Try to hold the rip shut with my bloody fingers. I come down that ladder. Get that bag settled quick onto a low shelf.

I lean down to see the thing that fell.

Matt hollers, "Buttle! *Don't! No! Leave it! Leave it!*"

I am looking at a wooden handle. I touch that first. And I know this thing. Know it well. I pick it up. I look at the blade. The row of teeth.

The handsaw. *Mine.*

I think, Wow. Been missing this for . . . like . . . two whole apple seasons. Or more? And the lieutenant . . .

he asked me questions. Like . . . did I throw this away . . . somewhere . . .

Mrs. Drinker comes into the garage. She says, "Hey, guys! Why all the shouting?" Moonie follows. He trots past her. Wags his whole self when he sees me. His nose finds the kibble. He starts cleaning that up.

But Matt is pointing a shaking finger at me. He is pale. Looks like he can hardly breathe. His words scrape up and out. He says, "He . . . he needs to get out of our garage!"

Mrs. Drinker says, "What? Matty?" Then she looks at me. Blood on my shirt. "Oh! Mason! You're hurt. You're hurt!"

I mean to tell her I am okay. But I cannot make the words. She rushes to me. Sees I'm holding the handsaw.

She says, "Mason!" She looks confused. And I am confused. She says, "W-where did this come from?"

I point up. Over my head. To the high shelf.

Matt cries, "No! No, it didn't!" He is shaking his head like wild.

Mrs. Drinker stares at her boy. Mouth open. She holds a tight fist to her chest.

I look around that garage. Tell you what. Everyone looks frozen.

I am pretty frozen too. Something is happening here. Everybody knows what. Everyone but me. I am begging myself inside of my brain, don't be stupid, Mason. Don't be stupid. You *need* to get this.

But I don't. I can't.

Lance is chin low. Hunched and still.

Corner of my eye I see Corey McSpirit by the small garage door. Tears pouring down his face. He is slow. Silent. He is backing himself out that door. His hand in one pocket. Then the square flash of his phone.

Just one thought comes: This handsaw must have got into the Drinkers' garage by way of nothing good.

chapter 67

THE LIEUTENANT'S PUZZLE

Mrs. Drinker comes to me. She takes that saw. Throws it on the low shelf. Like a log onto a fire. It clatters. Bounces. I put my hands on my ears.

She covers her face. Bends forward. Her body shakes. She is squeaking. Crying. She says, "No." She says that over and over again.

Matt cries, "No, Mom!" I look at his face. White. Scared. He says, "Stop! Stop it! Mom!"

Mrs. Drinker shakes her head. She cries, "My god, Matty! Oh. Matty! What did you do?"

And then I just know. Something I do not want to know. I push back on it. Hard.

I say, "Oh no. He could not. They could not . . . No.

It's all right. It's all right. No. No."

And I can't stop. And soon all I am saying is the same thing Mrs. Drinker is saying.

No. No. No.

Then I see the cruiser pull into the Drinkers' driveway. Blue and white. Sick blur. I see the officer. I see Corey McSpirit go to him. Feels like I am right beside him. I see the side of Corey's wet face. I see what he says. So clear. So slow.

Corey says, "They. Told. Me. They. Did. It."

I push words out of my throat. I say, "They couldn't have meant it! How could they know such a bad thing would happen? You can't know what you don't know!"

The officer comes closer. There is another cruiser in the driveway. My eyes go wild. Like they are shooting side to side in my head. I see all around inside the Drinkers' garage. All the walls are blurs and smears. White flashes of windows. Dark streaks in all the corners. I can't stop it. I see swishes of people. Some moving. Some close. Closer.

I say, "But they are kids! We are *all* just kids!"

There is a tug in my guts. I close my eyes. I am dropping. I am gravity. Going down. And I want to go. I want to be low. Then I am wrapped in huge arms. Bigger than my own.

Strange sound in my ear. I hear the voice say, "Mason. Oh my god, Mason. I am sorry. I'm so sorry."

The arms grow tighter. The voice goes to a whisper.

Who? I try to think. Who has this voice? I know it. But not this way. I know something hard. But this is soft. I open my eyes. The lieutenant. He has me. Like a cradle.

Then I know it. I'm getting sick. I turn to let it out. He holds me while it all comes up. He won't let go.

I choke and I tell him, "They didn't know. They couldn't know."

I wrap my fingers tight on his arm. I grip his sleeve.

I can hear me. Like some huge wounded wild thing. I hear me crying.

I say, "Nobody! Nobody meant to kill Benny Kilmartin!"

chapter 68

ONE WEEK GONE

The Drinkers are gone. I'm standing in their garage. I wonder if anything good has come of these days. We are one week gone from finding the handsaw. Word is probably going around: Mason Buttle is not the one. He played no trick. He made no mistake. Seems like all of this should feel better.

But tell you what. It's kind of like everything is still sad. I still feel it. Gray cloud over Merrimack.

Ms. Blinny helps. Lets me spend long days in the SWOOF. First day back she told me, "I have put extra time in my day. Time just for you, Mason Buttle."

I told her I could go tell it to the Dragon. She shook her head no. She sat down with me. She put her dry hands on top of my sweaty ones. She said, "Mason, you can tell this story to me."

So I did that. As best I could.

Now I'm staring at that greenish stain on the Drinkers' garage floor. The spot where I puked. Seems like I should get that off of there. Moonie follows me into the Drinkers' laundry room. I make a bucket of suds. Find a brush. I get started. Gross job. But the dog makes me smile. He tilts his head at what I'm doing. Looks at the brush like it might be a toy. I have to talk him out of that. I scrub and I think.

Funny thing. The lieutenant has been by the crumbledown. About every day. He even brought me a present. Brand-new handsaw. He will need to keep that old one. Probably for quite a while. And he took away the notebook and my Dragon pages. He read all that. Read it right about the same time I was here in this garage finding my old handsaw. That's what he said. Then he got the call to get down to the Drinker house. He said what I wrote fills him with understanding. Truths. He said, "I should have listened better, Mason."

He said something else. Sticks in my brain. He said, "Good families will help their children accept responsibility." He said that's all he can really say to us about the whole thing now. And Uncle Drum said that kind of means it's not really our business anymore.

Except for this: We love Benny Kilmartin. And we

hear things. Calvin read me the newspaper. Told about a break in the investigation. That was finding the handsaw. And it said the lieutenant feels grateful. But he still needs cooperation from several more Merrimack families. Calvin read, "There are individuals who have information."

We know who it means. Drinkers and Piersons.

I remember what Grandma said. She didn't hesitate to have me talk with the lieutenant. Well, pretty sure it is not the same for the Drinkers or the Piersons. We hear some things about them. Building up walls. Not stone walls like the one I built with Benny's dad Andy. Wall of people. Lawyers. Uncle Drum explained that part. He said they will get advice on how to keep the trouble away from their kids. He said the first thing they will do is *not* let their kids talk to the lieutenant. Another thing Uncle Drum said is this: The lieutenant has an impossible job.

Could be he is right.

Tell you what. The Drinkers sure did scoot right out of Merrimack. That is why I am here taking care of Moonie. Not sure for how long. Just know they are getting settled elsewhere. *Elsewhere* is what Mrs. Drinker said. Puts a fly in my head thinking about the day that Moonie will move away. But I'll take care of this dog same as I always have. Until they come for him.

One thing I told Ms. Blinny is how I think about everyone every day. She says that seems about right. Normal. It is what any person would do. I'll tell you who I feel bad about. Corey McSpirit. That's who. He had that secret in him. Not sure for how long. He is cooperating.

The *Merrimack Gazette* doesn't say the names. But it tells a story. It said the police believe two boys sawed on the rung of that ladder. Two means Matt and Lance. The paper said it started off as a prank. But then one boy went back. He did a lot more cutting. One boy means Matt. Might be he stayed around. In the orchard. Might be he saw Benny fall. Might be *he* was the last to see Benny alive. Then he took away evidence. Well. That evidence was my handsaw. Guess I left it out there in the orchard. By the tree fort. Wish I didn't.

Tell you what. I think on how bad I felt about not having the answers for the lieutenant. Bet you Corey felt double bad about keeping that secret inside. So Calvin and I already said it. If Corey comes back to school we will try to be his friends. We will sit by him on the bus.

I'm finished. Got my puke spot pretty well cleaned up. I rinse it all away. Chase the suds to the drain in the floor. Moonie and I watch the foam go down. His head tilts. Dog eyebrows twitch. Makes me smile.

I go in to wash up. I am welcome to hang out in the Drinker house. But tell you what. Doesn't feel right. There is the silence now. And I don't like the new-house smell here as much as I used to. I don't like that awful garage where it happened. I get Moonie out of here as much as

I can. Hate to leave him alone at night. But I make sure I come back to him first thing in the mornings. I come right after school too.

I put the bucket away in the Drinkers' laundry room. Leave it like I found it. I turn to Moonie. I say, "Wanna go apple picking, boy? Do ya? Let's go get a basket." I clap my hands. He jumps. And we get out of there.

chapter 69

FAMILY PLAN

I do not know what is up with Grandma. But she asked me to bring in this basket of apples. First time in a long time. And she told all of us to be at the table for a family meeting. Four o'clock sharp this afternoon. First time ever for that. She said, "Come with clean hands."

So here we are. Uncle Drum. Shayleen with her box of vanilla wafers. Grandma and me. And Moonie settling down by the legs of my chair. Grandma hands around paring knives and peelers. Tell you what. I didn't even know we had so many of them. That's what comes of not being allowed in the kitchen.

Well, she picks hers up. And an apple too. Deep red Rome. She starts taking the peeler to it. Then she gives us a look like we better get at it. And we do. Even Shay-leen, who has been looking at her peeler like it fell off some alien ship.

Grandma says, "We have a big pan to fill before any-one gets supper. We're making a crisp. And while we work, I have a few things for us all to think about." She takes a swallow. The peeler jingles in her hand. She says, "We've had hard times. Those kept coming for a while there. We were a bit knocked down. But now we have just gotten ourselves out from under an enormous weight. Lieuten-ant Baird has moved his investigation away from this family. With that put right . . ." Her voice squeaks a little. She says, "I think this is our time to ask ourselves to make some changes."

Then she tells how the Buttle farm belongs to family. Always has.

She says, "It is handed down to the next generation. We have had our share of losses. But we had two children. Drum and Mason's mom, Amy. With Amy gone, her part of the farm goes to her boy. So here at this table we have the two people who will inherit this house and land."

I forget to peel. I have never thought about living any-where besides here. But I never thought about it being half mine either.

Grandma catches me sitting still. She nods at my hands. Gets me peeling again. Shayleen starts to sniffle. She puts down her peeler. Blots her face in her elbow.

She sneaks a vanilla wafer. Like Grandma won't see that. Drum just keeps peeling and paring. Doesn't take his eyes off what he's doing.

Grandma says, "So, my men, you'll be partners in this place. But for now, it's mine. And Drum, that means no more selling off this land. I appreciate that you were managing things as well as you could. I'm glad there has been money. But you cannot go on shrinking a pie that doesn't belong wholly to you. That cannot be your job. And I can't force you to be an orchard man."

I think this: But he *is* an orchard man. I just know it.

Grandma says, "If apples are not your passion, fine. But you need a steady job, and much shorter days at the diner. Now, I have *my* plan. I'm going to start baking again. Small scale. Just as much as I want to put out for sale. No orders. It's the end of the season. But there are plenty of baking apples out there still. Now is a good time for me to try. So, Mason, I will be needing a good apple picker."

I say, "I can do it. I will love that."

She says, "And I'll be providing after-school care here. It's just one girl. She'll get off at the cluster stop with Mason. So there's a little more cash coming in, and a little more *life* happening around here."

I watch Grandma slice apples into the pan. She is quick. Bet she beats all of us three to one.

Grandma says, "Now, Shayleen. The shopping has to stop."

Tell you what. That girl turns into a puddle. Sobbing. Shoulders shaking. She has been ruining that vanilla wafer this whole time. Crumbs between her fingers. She looks at Drum. But he won't look at her. She says, "But I *have* to shop. I do." She has the black stuff running under her eyes. I hand the paper towels over.

Grandma shakes her head. She says, "You can't keep spending. You have to find a way to be a contributor."

Shayleen says, "How am I going to do that?"

Grandma says, "Well, you like to shop. Maybe you'd like to sell."

I say, "Yeah! Work at the stand. Sell apples. Sell pies. We can use the help. Holy cow, Shayleen! It'll get you outdoors."

Shayleen says, *"P-p-pies?"* She sputters that letter P all over the place. She says, "And then what? Someday Mason can just kick me out anyway?"

I say, "I can't kick you out!"

She says, "Yes, you could. You own half."

I say, "Well, then I could kick *half* of you out. But there's probably at least half of you that could do like Grandma says. Be a contributor." I tell Shayleen, "That half can stay."

Uncle Drum breaks out laughing. Big and loud. Not the usual at the Buttle house. Not the usual for him. Then I can't help it. I laugh too. Even Shayleen pouts and laughs at the same time. Grandma's shoulders shake. Minnow eyes shine.

I tell Shayleen, "Don't worry. We're going to find something for you to do. I don't know how it happened. Maybe just because you've been here so long. But you feel like family. Sort of. I don't think the Buttles can put family out."

Then we are quiet. Maybe like when everyone is just having their own thoughts. But the thing we get done together is that big pan of apples. Peeled. Pared. Full to the top.

Before supper, Uncle Drum and I go out and walk the orchard. Moonie too. He wanders up and back. Never far. Tell you what. I feel kind of mighty. About the place.

Half mine. Some day. Now there is something.

I ask Uncle Drum, "Do you know what job you want?"

He smiles. He says, "Not sure how much choice I have. But yeah. Grandma is right. I'm ready to work." He reaches up into the nearest tree. Pulls off a leaf or two. He looks them over. He says, "I'm proud of you for what you said to Shayleen."

I say, "Funny thing. Isn't it? Because that was no lie." We walk on, and I ask him, "Uncle Drum, how did we get Shayleen anyway? I mean, like, why did you bring her home?"

He says, "Well. I guess you could say, a weak moment

born of guilt. Do you know what that means?"

I say, "Well. Maybe if you tell me."

He says, "Six—almost seven years ago my little sister called me up late at night."

I say, "My mom?"

He says, "Yep. Amy. And she wanted a ride, is all. Her car broke down. Old bucket of bolts. She wouldn't get it fixed right and I was sick of that. She wanted me to come pick her up from the center of Merrimack after work. Third time in a week. And I didn't go. I said no. So she walked out into a foggy night. She got to Swaggertown Road. No sidewalks. Plenty of shadows and the fog, and, well, you know the rest. But what you don't know are the last words she ever said to me."

Uncle Drum stops. Looks at me.

He says, *"Thanks for nothing, Drum."*

I think this: I thought the stars were out that night. I don't know why. I just thought that. Then I think, somebody saying that, well, it would hurt pretty bad.

I say, "Sorry. It's hard, Uncle Drum."

He says, "Sure is. So when I saw this girl at the diner. Looking lost. In tears. Couldn't pay her tab. Well, I thought of Amy. Because you know, people are out there, Mason. People are just looking for one kindness."

I say, "So maybe it's not so much that other thing. The weak moment born of guilt. It's kindness. Like you said. Like give somebody a break, is all. And you did."

He nods. Smiles and claps a hand on my shoulder. He pushes me and pulls me and hugs me to him.

I say, "So hey, you think we can make Shayleen have a yard sale? Get that room cleaned out."

He says, "Yeah. I do. I think that's needed."

I say, "Good. Me too. And we don't have to feel bad about that, Uncle Drum. Because you know she doesn't know what she bought anyway. You know that, right?"

He says, "Yeah, I do. By the way, you want your room back?"

I think about all I can see from the upstairs window. The backyard. The orchard. The heap from the root cellar. And the mighty aurochs on his wall. I say, "Naw. Thanks, Uncle Drum. I'm good upstairs."

Then I tell him, "You know, I'm glad about what Grandma said tonight. To all of us. Because you know, I have had a bad feeling. Kind of like the Buttles were going to go extinct."

Uncle Drum snorts. He says, "I know what you mean."

I say, "I don't want that for us."

He says, "Won't happen. I promise you."

HOME BY A NOSE

When Uncle Drum and I come back up the orchard rows we smell apples baking. Cinnamon. And spice.

Uncle Drum says, "Nothing like being pulled home by your nose."

He is right about that. But I split off from him. Moonie too. We go down to the Drinker house so I can give the dog his supper. Settle him in for the night.

I get him fed. *Relieved.* I fill his water bowl and put National Public Radio on low. I hug him up. Scratch under his collar. I tell him how great he is. At the door I turn back. Like always. I feel so bad about leaving him alone. It has been a lot of nights now. Helps if I just see that he is curling up in his bed. Ready for a big sleep. But tonight, he doesn't do that.

He comes. Stands beside me. Nose by my knees. He looks up at me. I whisper, "Go to bed, boy. Don't you want to go to bed?" He waits.

I push the door open. About as wide as Moonie's nose. He stares at the space. I know I could back him up. Give him the *stay* hand. But I don't do that. I push the door wider. I step outside. Moonie steps out too. No dashing off. He waits while I close up the Drinkers' house.

I think this: If he turns back I'll go put him inside again.

So I start out. Moonie follows. Middle of the hill, he is still with me. Heading to the crumbledown. I smell the apples baking. Sugar and spice. And I think this: What dog wouldn't choose this home?

I let Moonie in ahead of me. And all eyes are on us. Grandma and Uncle Drum look worried.

I say, "He wanted to come. Feels awful down there." I point toward the Drinkers' house. I say, "And who knows when they're coming back? There's been nothing said about that. I don't want him to be lonely." I squat and wrap an arm around the middle of Moonie. I say, "This good dog . . . well . . . he did nothing wrong. He needs to be with me and I need to be with him. And I know. I know it is just until his family comes for him."

Saying all that gets me choked. I stop. Collect myself. It is how these days have been. Things piled up. Ache in the throat. It's rough.

I say, "I'm *not* going back down to the Drinker house anymore. I just can't."

Grandma nods. She says, "The dog is welcome here. Until . . ."

Uncle Drum says, "Sure. We'll take it day by day."

Shayleen says, "What about his food?"

I didn't think of that. But I don't want to go back for it.

Grandma says, "He can have egg and rice for breakfast. And then, we'll see."

Shayleen says, "We can get the real stuff delivered. UPS will bring it. Just saying."

At bedtime Moonie Drinker follows me up the stairs. He curls down right beside my bed. I hang one arm over. Inch it down until I touch him. He picks himself up. Hops onto the bed. He settles against me. And you can guess it. I let him stay.

chapter 71

ROW OF YELLOW BOARDS

On Saturday morning, I look out and see Andy Kilmartin. He is walking toward the crumbledown. He's bringing boards. On his shoulder. Looks like new ones. He lays them out by the porch. Turns to go back to the truck for more.

I pull the door open. Step out onto the sheet of plywood. It bumps and knocks on the joists below. Andy turns around. Then I don't know what to do. I mean to say hi. And more than that. But I just stand there.

Andy comes toward me. Steps up on the porch. The board rattles under both our feet. He wraps his arms around me. Tell you what happens. He cries his heart out. And all that time I feel his hands holding my back. Strong finger bones pull me in. Rock-wall fingers.

I am sweat. I am tears.

He sobs on my shoulder. Close to my ear.

He says, "I'm sorry. I am sorry, *son*."

And when Andy says that—says that word, *son*—it comes out in more sobs. When he breathes back in, it is like a high cry. Like one long note on a fiddle.

He says, "I forgot *who you are*, Mason. Franklin too. We are sorry. We got lost in our pain. And lost in this horrible, confused story. And missing our boy."

I cough it out. I say, "Same for me." It is about all I can say.

He says, "I am sorry. So, so sorry." He grips me hard. He says, "You sweet kid. You sweet, sweet kid."

When he lets me go I see the mark on his shirt. Big old sweat spot I made on Benny's poor dad. Moonie pushes between us. And it's good. Because we stoop down to pat him. And talk about him while we finish crying. We sit down. Legs hanging off the spot where the steps should be. We stick to words about good dogs. And great ones. And best ones.

Then Andy takes his hammer out of his tool belt. He leans down and starts pulling out the old nails. He knocks away bits of broken boards.

I say, "Can I do some? Can I work with you?"

Andy says, "Are you kidding? This is *your* job. I'm just here to help."

Uncle Drum comes out. Probably surprised. But he nods. Greets Andy. Then he asks, "How do those joists look?"

Andy says, "Still *serviceable*." And now he is the one who seems surprised.

Uncle Drum says, "Good to go then." He says, "Mason, think you can scare us up a couple of hammers?"

I hop to it. I have good luck with that. One in the shed. Another in the toolbox.

There's not much more talking. We work. All three of us. All picking nails. Then setting the new boards in. Spacing them right.

Done at midday. Rows of yellow boards shine. Baked pine in the sun. And I am glad when we move the mousey chair back. I figure we'll keep it. Just for Moonie Drinker. While he is here.

chapter 72

WHEN A DOG GOES HOME

I wake in the dark in my room upstairs. Moonie is standing *on* me. Two dog feet on my chest. Funny thing. He does step on me some. But just to get settled. Early on. Then he sleeps the night in a curl by my side. But now is the middle of the night. Or, I think so.

I whisper, "What, boy? What is it?"

He hops off me. Off the bed. He stands with front feet up on the window sash. I sit up. Look out across the orchard. And down the hill.

I see it. Small square of light. A window. Then I know it. Somebody is home inside the Drinkers' house.

I whisper Moonie back into the bed. I hold him. Tuck my nose into the soft coat. I breathe him in. I pat the spotted back. I stroke the white belly. I feel his breath in my ear. Reaches down to my middle.

I think this: Hard day coming.

I wait for dawn. I know I have to do right. I get up. Get dressed. Moonie rests on the bed. On top of warm sheets. His head between his paws. He watches me with his golden-brown eyes.

I keep my shoes quiet on the stairs. But Moonie clicks going all the way down. Toenails. Toenails. Toenails.

I hear somebody say, "*Psst!* Mason!"

I say, "Holy cow!" I about jump from my skin. I say, "Hush! Shayleen!"

She says, "There's a lady out there. She's been sitting in a minivan."

I peek out. Don't you know. It is Mrs. Drinker. Come for her dog.

First thing is, I wave Shayleen back into her room. I will do this. But on my own.

Moonie waits at my legs. I breathe a big breath in, and it shakes all the way out. I say, "Well, boy. Come on now." Moonie wags. I try not to let him know what today means. Try not to let him know why my heart feels heavy. Like the head of a hammer.

Got my hand on our doorknob. I peek again. And I see Mrs. Drinker. Out of the car now. She's opening the big sliding door.

I think this: I should open our door. Let Moonie

run. Let him fly. Let him go wherever home will be. *Else-where*. But I stand there. Bite my lip.

Then I see. Mrs. Drinker. Turning around from the car. She is hefting something out. The bin full of dog food. Got some papers on top of it. The pages flutter. October wind.

I watch and I watch. And I sure do wonder what she is doing. She comes and sets the bin down on the new deck boards. She goes back to the car and hauls out Moonie's dog bed. She puts it with the bin and slides everything a little bit closer to our door. My heart thuds.

Mrs. Drinker turns to leave.

I think this: She is right there. And I'm right here. Feels like watching a friend walk away. What about Moonie?

I open the door. Step out on the fresh yellow porch boards. She doesn't seem to hear me. I could still slip back inside . . .

I say, "Mrs. Drinker?"

She turns around. Moonie bolts past me. Springs toward her. Tail wagging. Body wiggling. It is his greeting for ones he loves the most.

She crouches to catch his ruff in her hands. She hugs the dog and says, "Oh, Mason. I thought your house was still sleeping."

I say, "We are waking up."

She smiles. The sad kind. She fidgets. Strokes Moonie's coat. Her eyes are full of water. Makes me wonder if our porch is a crying place.

I say, "I'm sorry about letting him sleep here. It wasn't the whole time. And I'm not trying to steal him."

She says, "Oh, no, no. I'm so glad he wasn't alone." She says, "Mason, we have troubles. You know that." She chokes up. She says, "And we think Moonie will do best if he can stay with you."

I wonder what *stay* means.

She is nodding her head. Then she says, "For always."

My heart pumps. I see pink in the air. It hangs there.

She says, "He thinks he is yours anyway." She laughs a tiny laugh. "We think he chose you. Both Matty and I think it." She says, "This dog is a love. And he deserves love. You are his home. So there's his food and his vet records. And the bed. All you need."

I think this: Moonie is mine. That pink wash blooms again.

I say, "Thank you!" It comes up all dusty. But I mean it. I say, "There's no better gift. No gift like Moonie."

She says, "I think this dog loved you from the day you sailed into the cellar. He must have thought, that boy is spectacular!"

We each send one little laugh into the early air.

I say, "Mrs. Drinker, it's not my business. But I'm sorry. About the troubles."

She nods. Frowns. Then her face breaks.

I say, "But maybe I can tell you this. It will be okay. Someday. Somehow. Don't you think?"

She sighs to get her breath. She is crying streams of tears. She says, "Right now . . . I don't see how. But I will hope for that. My god. I will."

Then she hugs me and she hugs Moonie. She tells him, "Be a good boy for Mason." He kisses her. Good-bye.

She gets into her van. I keep Moonie close. Hold him. Hope he won't be confused. But he is. He cries. Little murmurs I can feel from his chest. He is marching on his paws. I tell him, "I know, I know. But you have me. Promise you, boy. I promise."

We watch the van roll away. Not easy to sort out. My heart feels scrambled. Mrs. Drinker is gone. Don't think she is coming back to Merrimack.

But Moonie is settling down in my arms. Like he gets it. He's staying. Forever.

chapter 73

APPLE CRISP

Tell you what. We got four people peeling and paring again. Grandma's apple crisp was good. We are making another. Apple-cinnamon Sunday inside the crumble-down. And this pan is a big one. Got some people coming over. First time for that in a long time.

Uncle Drum asked for some help. He bought a bunch of pairs of work gloves down at Bishell's Hardware. Plan is, we will haul that heap out of the root cellar site. Load it into Uncle Drum's truck. Dump run on Monday.

Soon the apples are baking. The lieutenant arrives. Then Calvin Chumsky and his parents come down Jona-gold Path. Sun shining on them. They want to help. And they want to see what is left of our Caves of Lascaux.

They wheel Calvin in the chair. He is wearing both his tan-sandy shoes. He can walk again. Some. But the dead-asleep leg is still waking. And hurting. And making him tired. But Calvin is his same self as always on the inside. Mighty.

I help push him around back to the dip in the yard. Moonie dances close to my heels. Beside Calvin's wheels.

Calvin sighs to see the great aurochs on the open cellar wall. He says, "Oh... how different to see him standing out in the light." He turns wide eyes on me. Then on the cellar again. The Chumsky parents stare too.

Calvin's mom says, "Oh, the animal is beautiful. Powerful!" She squints. She says, "I can imagine how the whole root cellar was. The roof. The shaft. It must have been an *enchanting* place to be. So old. So rare!"

Mr. Chumsky nods. "Looks like a lot of dirt. And a lot of fun. And, hey, a lesson in engineering! How will you boys top that? What's your next project?"

Lieutenant Baird hears that. He rolls his eyes. Uncle Drum makes a low sound in his throat. But then everyone is laughing.

We put on the gloves. Face the heap. We start at the top. Lift out old boards. And long strings of brambles. And the work goes well.

Calvin has to sit. Just watching. But he likes it. He checks out all the parts when we walk them by on the way to the truck.

He says, "There! That has to be one of the capping pieces. Look at the old spike that held it in place. There's the board we cut the circle from."

I say, "Calvin! Remember? That circle hit me right in the lip!" I make it sound funny. I make people laugh.

I tug a pretty long board out of the heap. Push that behind me as I go. I feel the weight lift. Got help on the other end. I look. It is the lieutenant. We carry that board. Toss it up on the truck. Tell you what. One more thing in Merrimack feels a little closer to all right.

When the big stuff is gone we switch to shovels and rakes. Out comes the old rag rug. Two five-gallon buckets. Both busted and cracked. We sweep to get the last of it clean. Hard dirt and dust.

Something shows up there on the pale painted floor. Charcoal lines. And I know the shape. I know what it is.

I shout, "Calvin! It is your dead man! Dead man with the bird head!"

Well, don't you know it. Everyone comes to see. And Calvin tells how it worked. How the shaft put light on that little stick drawing of a man. How Calvin drew him. True and important. Like the dead man in the Caves of Lascaux.

He tells and I listen. Then I take a step out. I look up. Have to squint at the bright round sun today. What I feel is this: the loving memory of Benny. Benny who told me beams of sunlight will take you up to heaven.

Grandma comes down with the hot apple crisp. Pot holders wrapped around that wide baking pan. And Shayleen comes behind her. Shayleen *outdoors*! She carries the dishes. Runs back for spoons and cream.

We pull off our work gloves. The crisp is served. Passed all around. Noses breathe in. Deep and long. Then every spoonful melts in every mouth.

Uncle Drum says, "Gift from the orchard." He looks out to the trees.

I say, "And from Grandma."

The bowls are scraped clean. Then funny thing. It is Shayleen who stands looking long and hard at the cellar. Clean, square hole with stony walls. One aurochs, one dead man. She says, "You boys sure made a *ruin*!"

But Calvin is smiling. He says, "Actually, it's a *relic*."

Don't know why but I guess it's not surprising. I like the sound of what Calvin said better.

chapter 74

LAST APPLE

Late October comes to the orchard. I'm thinking about winter. Because it will come too. These rows will rest. Snow will fall.

I get an idea about sledding down the back hill. I think I can put the blade on the tractor. Go down and bank up the snow. Keep us from skidding into those yards. Down at the bottom. See, I cleaned out the shed for progress. Deep in the back I found our two old sleds. One was Uncle Drum's. The other was my mom's. And I can see it. We'll go doubles. Calvin and Corey on one—because I hope he will come over. And me on the other—and you won't believe this, but Annalissetta Yang too. Turns out she is the after-school-care girl. The one that Grandma helps now. Uncle Drum and I built a ramp onto the new porch. Did that together. Annalissetta gets in and out of the crumbledown on her own just fine. Pretty sure she can go sledding. Like, if we leave her Crocodile walker at the top of the hill. Then I can pull her back up again. I will ask first. But I know this: She will sure like to go fast.

Well. Easy for me to get ahead of myself. There is no snow yet.

So for now, I walk with this dog of mine. Best one in the world. High tail and curious. Seems like he is pretty happy with me. I reach up and pull down an apple. Last one on this tree. The season is pretty much past. I roll it for Moonie. Good and hard down the row. That dog loves to go. Ears back. Hind legs pumping. And I think this: How good it must feel. Digging in like he does. Paws and toenails hitting earth. Belly skimming that yellow grass.

Moonie Buttle has his eyes, nose, and heart on just one thing: that last apple. What a dog loves.

Gets me thinking. I know what I love too. Family and friends. All the ones here and all ones gone. I love my dog, and this orchard, and a crumbledown house.

Funny thing. The way that feels. It's not dark, unlucky, or stupid. Tell you what. Stupid can go sit on the head of a pin somewhere.

Knowing what you love is smart.

ACKNOWLEDGMENTS

It occurs that the writer and the orchardist have something in common: both learn to prune judiciously. It can also be said that both do well to surround themselves with like-minded friends who carry sharp and helpful tools.

On that very point, I'm fortunate to count these brilliant, creative women in my community of writers: Sandi Shelton, Nancy Hall, Doe Boyle, Leslie Bulion, Mary-Kelly Busch, Lorraine Jay, Kay Kudlinski, Judy Theise, Nancy Elizabeth Wallace, Ali Benjamin, Molly Burnham, Jackie Davies, Lita Judge, Grace Lin, Lynda Mullaly Hunt, Cammie McGovern, and Kimberly Newton Fusco. You are the stars inside my sliced apples. My heartfelt thanks to all of you.

Katherine Tegen, I am forever grateful to be published by your imprint. Thanks for leading the hardworking team that takes such good care of every page of every project—you are all the best! And thank you, Katherine, for our friendship.

Miriam Altshuler, I'm so grateful that you took me on. Thanks for your guidance and friendship.

Thank you to the Fan brothers for the stunningly gorgeous cover art (it's like you were there!) and to Amy Ryan, senior art director at HarperCollins Children's Books.

Bushel baskets of thanks to:

Valerie Pierce-Grove for notes on using voice-recognition computer programs.

Amanda and Merry Marrone for generously sharing your experiences so that I could better understand the character Annalissetta Yang.

Mary J. Elliott for sharing your knowledge and skill as an EMT, particularly notes on the fine art of extrication.

Diane Blinn, who showed me by example the daily warmth and caring that happens in a school social work office.

Gail Brown, who, along with Deb Sternklar, hosted my two all-time favorite library visits up in Voorheesville, New York.

My writing dogs, Luna, Broomis, and Atticus (my "Moonie Drinker" dog), for sitting on me until the work is done.

My family—near, far, and right under the roof—without your good love there'd be no shiny apples in my life. Jonathan, Sam and Kristy, Marley and Ian, all the Petrequins, Peards, Pierce-Groves, Buellers, Caufields, Rices, and Youngs, thanks for your support. I love you back with all my heart! Same to my Schmidt-Goetzes, for you are my extended family.

Finally, love and thanks to my uncle Dick, who once dug a cellar out from under his house. (How could I *not* believe that all things are possible after that?) You are my Mike Mulligan. I miss you.

More from award-winning author
LESLIE CONNOR

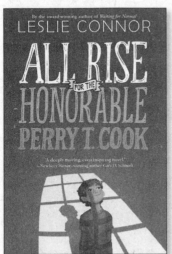